Twinkle!

The Ultimate Guide to Outdoor Christmas Decorating

DARREN VADER

NORTH POLE PRESS

You are a *Memory Maker.*

It's the most important job in the world.

Twinkle: The Ultimate Guide to Outdoor Christmas Decorating

First Edition 2024
North Pole Press
info@iam.christmas

For my mother, Carol.

You gave me the hope that I love sharing with the world.

North Pole Alert!

Legal Disclaimer

Hold onto your elf hats, folks! Before we dive into the glittery abyss of holiday cheer, we need to address something. Decorating like a pro often means dancing with danger—think ladders, rooftops, tangled lights, and possibly some acrobatics that would make a circus performer blush. Yep, I'm talking about using tools at height and getting cozy with other potentially perilous situations.

Let's be real: Every year, despite the merriest of intentions, people do indeed find themselves in the ER or worse because of holiday decorating mishaps. So, here's the deal. The tips and tricks outlined in this book come with a glowing and flashing caution sign. By diving into this guide, you acknowledge the risks involved.

Neither the author nor any individual or entity named in this book or associated with this festive tome's writing, publishing, selling, or marketing can be held responsible for how you apply the information shared. Your safety is paramount, so proceed cautiously and maybe keep a medical professional on speed dial.

Lights run on electricity, and electricity can be as dangerous as a bus without brakes. So, take it slow, channel your inner tortoise, and remember: If something seems dangerous, it probably is. Trust your gut!

Always follow the manufacturer's instructions for lights, ladders, and other equipment. The folks behind this book - the author, publisher, and whoever else got roped into this project - have no idea what gear you're working with. We don't know if your building/home is older than Saint Nick or if you're trying to decorate while also having a few frosty ones, and we don't mean the snowman. Please don't! Hence, we can't promise we've covered every safety tip under the sun, nor can we guarantee that following any steps or guidance outlined in this book will lead to a picture-perfect or incident-free decorating season.

Happy decorating, and may the glitter be ever in your favor!

"Nothing says 'holiday spirit' like nearly breaking your neck to outshine your neighbor's inflatable Santa. If you're not risking life and limb, are you even decorating?"

Shawn Tacina, Tacina Family Light Show

"Hanging Christmas lights is a contact sport, and decorators are the Olympians of holiday cheer. When your house can be seen from the International Space Station, you know you've done it right!"

Gerald Thomson, Veteran Decorator

Foreword

A Sprinkle of Inspiration From Chuck Smith

I remember, as a kid, riding around town with the entire family and looking at Christmas lights. Somehow, I got it in my head that Santa would miss our house if it weren't decorated, so I begged my dad to buy some lights. He kept forgetting, so I saved my money and bought a string of official Christmas lights. I remember it like it was yesterday, even though it was 60+ years ago. The big spend of $2.99 at the corner drugstore got me 15 C9 multi-color bulbs: red, green, blue, white, and some weird shade of yellow. Each year, I'd struggle with where to hang those lights so Santa wouldn't miss the house. It must have worked because presents were always under the tree on Christmas morning.

Years later, I started dreaming of living in that one house in the neighborhood with the most decorations. I "borrowed" ideas from other Christmas displays and stumbled onto using a computer for flashing the lights in patterns, eventually leading to the lights dancing to music. The more my decorating evolved, the more cars would be parked in front of the house to see what I had created. Christmas decorating became a year-round hobby for me.

In December, I'd walk up and down my street listening to people, and that's when I learned my hobby had become a Christmas tradition for countless families. They would comment on the new stuff I'd added to the display, old stuff that I had moved around, and about remembering a particular prop from years before. Everyone was always happy.

I realized my little holiday decorating hobby was making positive, lifelong memories for thousands of others. Most people can't say that, but I can, and I'm proud of it.

My over-the-top display was becoming a big deal in my town while the Internet was becoming recognized as valuable. I created a website called PlanetChristmas.com to share details of my display and to create a community for decorators to exchange ideas. Soon, there was an active forum, magazine, merchandise, and even a trade show.

The PlanetChristmas website has faded as the world moved to a few major social media players. The trade show still exists and is called Christmas Expo. Local gatherings are now common and called "Minis" because they're smaller versions of the original PlanetChristmas-inspired trade show.

Now, if you're thinking about dazzling the neighborhood and showing off your skills, what's the best way to decorate as you strive to be a holiday hero? Your imagination is the only limitation, so get ready to pull some great ideas from this book. Twist them a bit to add your own personality, and prepare to see smiles on countless faces during the holiday season.

I still decorate, though not nearly as grand as the good old days. Adults regularly come up to me, saying how they remember, as a child, when their whole family made a special trip just to see my house every year. Now, that's a lifelong memory!

It's your turn. Get to work!

Chuck Smith
Proud Christmas decorator
www.SantaChuck.com
www.planetchristmas.com

Contents

Introduction

Welcome to **Twinkle: The Ultimate Guide to Outdoor Christmas Decorating!** If you've ever dreamed of transforming your front yard into a dazzling wonderland that could make Santa's North Pole operation blush, you're in the right place.

Decking the halls and everything else isn't just a festive pastime; it's a bold declaration of your holiday spirit. In a world where inflatable Santas and synchronized light shows reign supreme, holiday decorating has become an Olympic sport of sorts.

At some point, we've all dived headfirst into holiday decorating, only to end up tangled in lights that refuse to stay lit, wrestling with garland that insists on sliding down the porch columns, or, heaven help us, taking an unscheduled dive off the ladder!

That's where this book comes in! These pages are packed with everything you need to know to design, plan, install, troubleshoot, take down, maintain, and properly store your outdoor Christmas display yourself—and do it with enthusiasm and confidence!

What qualifies me as your guide on your quest to be the next contestant on The Great Christmas Light Fight? I've been in the Christmas lighting and design business for about three decades. Before that, I was an avid decorator with an extreme light show. I am the founder of Extreme Lightscapes – a production services company that designs and installs large-scale synchronized light, music, and special effect shows for commercial clients worldwide. I'm also the founder of The Christmas Light Emporium, an online store preferred by decorators for our unique LED light colors and our wide selection of Christmas lights, decor, and installation accessories. I'm on a mission to help decorators create more smiles, memories, and joy through Christmas decorating.

Whether you're a traditionalist who favors classic wreaths and elegant strings of warm white lights (er, I mean, 2800 kelvin – more on that later) or an enthusiast who dreams of being the next contestant on The Great Christmas Light Fight, this book is for you. Inside, you'll find all the crucial knowledge, instructions, guidance, expert tips, and creative ideas to help you safely and proudly design and install a festive masterpiece that will make lasting holiday memories, create as many smiles as possible, and elevate your home's festive appeal to the status of neighborhood legend.

It's time to roll up your sleeves, channel your inner Clark W. Griswold, and get ready to dazzle.

The Christmas Decorators Pledge

I solemnly swear, as a responsible Christmas decorator and Memory Maker, to uphold the following truths:

1. I will learn to define the color of my LED Christmas lights by their Kelvin temperature and color wavelength and will stop using terms like "warm white" and "cool white" as color specifications. They are not. I may as well be asking for "fruit cake" colored lights. See "Common Terms You Need to Know"

2. I understand that mixing the color temperatures of the same-colored lights within my display is like putting pineapple on pizza, and I won't do it. Not ever.

3. I will never use a light string as an extension cord to jump from a bush to a tree. Nope, not even once. Ever. I might as well use spaghetti for shoelaces.

4. I promise not to turn my front yard into a chaotic carnival of mismatched lights just because they were 90% off at the big box stores. My family deserves better than something from a clearance aisle horror story.

5. I will resist the temptation to shine a floodlight into my neighbor's windows—unless, of course, they still owe me money. Then all bets are off. Heck, I'm probably already doing that.

6. I will wrap my extension cords with the precision of a neurotic artist, ensuring they don't morph into knots that only a wizard could untangle.

7. I have come to terms with the fact that yard gnomes will never be elves, so I'm officially retiring the red-and-white hats. It's a tough pill to swallow, but hey, someone's got to keep these gnomes grounded in reality.

8. I promise not to ignore those glaring danger signs and use the top of my ladder as a step, even if it feels like a shortcut to hanging lights like a festive superhero. Just because Santa can glide nimbly across the rooftops doesn't mean I need to try and match him.

9. I will make sure Santa Claus stays out of the nativity scene. And Charlie Brown is not one of the three wise men. Also, Baby Yoda is not an acceptable replacement to lay in the manger if I can't find an actual baby Jesus.

10. I will keep the number of lights under seven digits and my spending below Madagascar's GNP. Otherwise, the family accountant might stage an intervention, and nobody wants that kind of holiday drama, right?

11. That said, I understand that there's no such thing as "too many Christmas lights." If your house isn't visible from space, are you even trying?

Chapter One

Christmas Lights Can Change the World

Smiles + Memories + Joy = Hope. That's my life's equation. It also drives my company, The Christmas Light Emporium, to help decorators like you create as many smiles and memories as possible. **You're the Memory Makers**. You're on the front line, crafting holiday displays that bring joy, spark smiles, create memories, and ultimately sprinkle more hope into this crazy world. While doctors, lawyers, accountants, and Elon Musk might roll their eyes, I believe that Christmas decorating is, hands down, the most important job in the world. A smile is a powerful agent of change. *You are the creators of smiles, the memory makers, and the much-needed agents of hope.*

Lighting is magical, plain and simple. Primitive man worshiped the moon for its ability to light up the night, the sun for its warmth, and fire for extending daylight into the darkness. He also worshiped crushing your enemies, seeing them driven before you, and hearing the lamentations of their women if Conan the Barbarian is to be believed. But that's a different story. Throughout history, lighting in all its forms has been a source of inspiration and enlightenment. It warms us, makes us happy, and fuels creativity. It sparks conversations and storytelling, bringing us closer together. It makes us smile as memories are made. It's the twinkle in our eyes that represents hope. Lighting brings us hope.

I've witnessed the magic of Christmas lights in action countless times. I've seen the twinkle of hope not just in children's eyes but also on the faces of adults. It's like a doorway to the past for them. Lighting brings us hope. This passion sparked decades ago when I started installing an outrageously huge computer-controlled light show at my home. I watched children dance and sing, their eyes twinkling with joy. I saw adults with blank expressions staring at me in my Santa suit like I'd lost my marbles, only to see my happiness reflected in their own eyes. Hope. I was bringing hope to my community.

I could tell you about the single mom who visited our Christmas lights every night with her autistic son because it kept him calm. Or the countless Memory Makers who create elaborate light displays and raise donations for various charities. Or the homeless man who gets his winter clothing each year thanks to Christmas lights. Or the small food bank near my home, benefiting from the generosity of those who visit our display and others in the area. People give because they recognize the value in what we do. We're giving people hope.

I could share stories of adults bringing their senior parents to see Christmas lights, a cherished tradition that reminds them of their youth and fills them with joy and hope.

The magic of lighting extends beyond Christmas. It's a focal point at weddings, backyard BBQs, parties, concerts, homes, buildings, public art, museums, roadways—the list goes on. Lighting elicits a strong emotional response in every setting it graces. But I'm no expert in architectural lighting or illuminating public roadways. I stick to what I know: holidays, events, parties, and patios. I focus on places where lighting can bring people together, make them smile, bring them joy, create memories, and offer a glimmer of hope. As Memory Makers, I hope you'll join me.

Darren Vader

Decorator, Memory Maker, Entrepreneur, Traveler, Author

Chapter Two

The Great Christmas Light Fight

Do You Have What It Takes to Be a Contestant on The Great Christmas Light Fight?

Back when I started decorating, my family thought I was crazy. You see, I didn't do anything small. My display was huge and synchronized to music. It grew bigger every year. I even convinced four neighbors to include their homes in the light show. On the weekends closer to Christmas, we had lines of cars for about a mile in each direction. We collected donations for a local food bank and filled their cupboards every December. News crews visited almost every weekend.

Then, I heard about a new network television show about extreme Christmas displays that was about to debut on ABC. I remember thinking to myself, "Nobody's going to watch that! It will never make it past season one!" Well, that was more than a decade ago. I've now helped several clients prepare to be on the show, and nearly everyone who has been a constant is someone I call a friend.

David Peace is one of those friends. He also happens to be the head elf at Experience Lights, where he designs light show controllers, including the GFade 8 that I'll talk about later in this book, as well as a complete line of synchronized light show controllers for RGB light shows and lots of other fun inventions. If you're interested in learning more about Experience Lights, visit their website here: https://experiencelights.com

But this story isn't about David's work life; it's about his family's experience as contestants on a network show that I thought would only last one season.

My name is David Peace. In 2017, I received an unexpected email from a casting producer of ABC's "The Great Christmas Light Fight" regarding a YouTube video I had posted of our home's Christmas light show. Initially, I thought it was a scam, given the email came from a random Gmail address. However, after some research, I realized it was genuine and soon got in touch with the producers.

The process moved quickly. We had a Skype interview that summer, and by October, we were notified that our family had been selected to be filmed in December of that same year.

After a mountain of paperwork, calls with legal, and swearing an oath to ABC and its affiliates, we started preparing for what was sure to be an exciting journey. We were assigned a segment producer whose job was to ensure our family and our display looked their best for television. While some of their critiques were tough, we reminded ourselves that this was for a TV show, and we had to set aside some of our opinions. Navigating the legal requirements was challenging—we had to deal with music licensing, character licensing, and getting approvals for using CO_2 effects.

Once everything was cleared legally, the day of filming finally arrived. Just 30 minutes before our judge, Taniya Nayak, was scheduled to arrive, everything started to go wrong. The light show wasn't functioning as expected, creating an incredibly stressful situation. I frantically rebuilt all the show files, reconfigured everything at lightning speed, and copied all the necessary files.

When Taniya finally arrived, it was time for the big reveal. At that moment, I was about 50/50 on whether the light show would work as planned. Watching the episode, you can see my immense relief when the lights turned on.

Filming on judging day was long and exhausting, continuing into the early hours of the next morning. Despite the challenges, we loved our crew, who were incredibly kind and welcoming. Taniya was an absolute delight, and everyone involved with the show, especially the producers, were class acts. While we didn't expect to win (and we didn't), the experience was truly memorable. Our kids still talk about it as a cherished family memory to this day.

David Peace, Peace Family Light Show

If you'd like to learn more about the Peace family's love of Christmas decorating, check out their website at https://www.peacefamilylights.com

Chapter Three

The Basics

I remember a time when I didn't know much about Christmas decorating. I started small. I loved decorating my Christmas tree every year. Before I was married, I was the only single guy I knew who bought a real Christmas tree and spent a week decorating it every year. Fast forward a decade or two. Imagine pulling up to the check-out stand at Home Depot with a shopping cart completely piled high and overflowing with extension cords. That was me. That's how I reacted when I finally figured out how to make my Christmas lights dance to music. I hadn't figured out all the details at that point. But I knew I would need a TON of extension cords. All of them, in fact. Every extension cord in that Home Depot. I was flying high as I started my quest for holiday hero status. Don't be like me.

Instead of jumping off a cliff like I did, let's start at the beginning. Get ready for an exhilarating journey into the world of Christmas light decorating jargon. WHOOOP! Consider this your exclusive pass to the enchanting realm of holiday illumination. Mastering these terms will not only make you the star of your next festive gathering, but it will also ensure your dazzling display remains drama-free.

This is a pretty long list. If you find your eyelids getting heavy, feel free to skip to the next chapter and flip back here when you need to.

Common Terms You Need to Know:

– A –

Ampere (Amps): If "amps" had you scratching your head, meet its formal name—Ampere. It's the superstar unit of electric current, named after a French guy, André-Marie Ampère, who I like to imagine had a massive feud with James Watt over whose name carried the greater charge. Unfortunately, that probably wasn't the case since Watt died in 1719 and Ampere wasn't born until 1775, but a guy can dream, right? Imagine your electrical system as a busy highway: the ampere measures how many cars (the electric charges) zoom past a point in one second. So, it's basically traffic control for electrons. Knowing the ampere rating of your Christmas lights and following all manufacturer recommendations for maximum amp ratings means you won't fry your circuits and end up calling an electrician right in the middle of your holiday merriment.

AWG: see "Wire Gauge": AWG is an abbreviation for "American Wire Gauge."

– B –

Bulb Base: This is the part of the bulb that screws into the socket, making sure your little twinklers get the juice they need to shine bright like the holiday star they are. There are different sizes of bases, such as E12 (candelabra) and E17 (intermediate). These are not to be confused with R2 or BB8 from Star Wars, although an army of them lighting up your yard would be pretty epic.

– C –

C7 Bulb: This little gem is just the right size for those who want their holiday lights to be noticeable but not blindingly obvious from space. The C7 bulb is about 1.5 inches long, making it a medium-sized option perfect for outlining your home's architectural features or adorning Christmas trees if you're going for that vintage, classic vibe. With their E12 base, these bulbs are the quintessential middle child in the world of holiday lighting.

C9 Bulb: If the C7 is the more reserved sibling, the C9 bulb is the one who steals the show at family gatherings. At a larger 2.25 inches long, these bulbs are the go-to choice for roof outlines. C9s have an E17 base and are ideal for impactful outdoor displays like roof lines and large tree wraps. They're the 'go big or go home' option of the holiday lighting world and the most common size of bulb used by decorators

Candelabra (E12 Bulb Base): Another name for a C7 or E12 socket size. It can also refer to the size of the base of the bulb. The term "candelabra" primarily refers to the E12 bulb base, commonly found in decorative and functional lighting. In the world of Christmas lights, candelabra bases are most often paired with C7 bulbs. This particular size is favored for its ability to balance elegance and practicality, making it ideal for a variety of festive applications, from classic Christmas tree lights to enchanting outdoor displays. The candelabra base ensures a secure fit into the socket, providing reliable and consistent illumination without the need for frequent adjustments. In the broader realm of lighting, candelabra bases are also used in chandeliers and other fixtures that require a touch of sophistication.

Cherry Picker: a type of man lift commonly used for installing Christmas lights to the top of large trees, steeply pitched roof ridges, and other perilous locations. Big box hardware stores or commercial equipment rental companies can rent them. Just do a Google search for "man lift," "bucket lift," or "cherry picker" rental. If you have the budget and large trees you want to wrap to the top, having a cherry picker at your disposal will ensure you can get the job done safely.

Clips/Christmas Light Clips: Used to secure Christmas light strings onto a home or building. Christmas light clips are those nifty little gadgets that keep your twinkling masterpieces securely attached to your home so they don't end up in your neighbor's yard, the stomach of your neighbor's dog, or worse, forming a tangled, horrifying mess on your roof. Christmas light clips come in various shapes and sizes, each designed to help you attach various sizes, types, and shapes of lights and strings to gutters, shingles, railings, brick, or any other architectural feature you want to illuminate. Think of them as the backstage crew for your holiday display, working tirelessly to make sure everything stays in place while you bask in the glory of your decorative genius. So next time you admire your perfectly aligned lights, give a nod to those Christmas light clips—they've earned it.

Color Temperature: Ever wondered why some white Christmas lights make your home look like a cozy log cabin while others give off the vibe of an alien spaceship landing? That's all thanks to color temperature, measured in Kelvin (K). I know what you're thinking right now. You're thinking about the time you had to learn about Kelvin in eighth-grade science and blew it off because you were never going to use it in the real world. Well, welcome to the real world, buddy. Population: You. Here's your official refresher course. The lower the Kelvin number, the warmer and cozier the white light feels—which is perfect for making your living room look like a Hallmark movie set. I'm talking about that golden, warm glow that's below 3000 K. On the flip side, those higher Kelvin numbers of white light (above 5000 K) give you a crisp, cool light that can make your yard sparkle like Elsa's Ice Palace. Understanding color temperature is the key to setting the right festive mood. Whether you want your house to look warm and inviting or cool and modern, you've got to pick the right temperature for your white lights. Learning to think about your favorite white color in terms of its color temperature (Kelvin) is the only way you can consistently match your colors of whites throughout your display. This is particularly true of LED lights, which are available in a much wider spread of color temperature than incandescent lights

Color Wavelength: Alright, let's get a bit science-y for a moment. "Color wavelength" refers to the distance between successive peaks of a wave of light, measured in nanometers (nm). Each color in the visible spectrum corresponds to a specific range of wavelengths. For instance, red light has a longer wavelength, usually around 620-750 nm, which might explain why it's the chill, laid-back elder sibling of the colors. On the other end, violet light has shorter wavelengths, around 380-450 nm, making it the hyperactive kid giving off those high-energy vibes. Understanding color wavelengths is crucial, especially if you're mixing different types of lights. You want to avoid a color clash that could rival a bad 80s fashion show, so matching wavelengths ensures your vibrant holiday display is coordinated and visually pleasing. In the world of LED lighting, the basic colors, like red, green, and blue, are typically pretty close in color wavelength from all manufacturers. However, colors like teal, pink, purple, yellow, and others can have varying color wavelengths from one manufacturer to the next. So, knowing what wavelength your preferred color is will help you maintain consistent color throughout your display, even if you are using LED lights from multiple manufacturers.

Commercial/Commercial Grade: A grade of lighting or decor/accessory, etc., that is manufactured to tighter specifications, using higher quality materials, etc., than an economy option and is designed to withstand harsh outdoor environments better. Unlike your average economy stuff that cries at the sight of a rain cloud, these bad boys laugh in the face of harsh weather. They're built tough, like the Chuck Norris of holiday decor.

Cool White vs. Warm White Christmas Lights: Ah, the age-old debate of cool white versus warm white Christmas lights, the rock stars of the festooning world. Imagine cool white lights as the edgy, modern cousins with their crisp, icy glow—perfect if you're aiming for a winter wonderland straight out of a minimalist's dream. These lights usually have a color temperature above 5000 K, giving off a clean, almost clinical brightness that's fantastic for outdoor displays looking to shine like a winter night's sky. Now, warm white lights are their cozier, more traditional counterparts, radiating a golden, inviting hue. Think of them as the soft embrace of a log cabin fireplace, with color temperatures below 3000 K. They're ideal for indoor settings or for those who want to add a touch of nostalgic charm to their holiday decor. See "Color Temperature."

Cutters: (see "Dikes")

– D –

Dikes (Cutters): No, I'm not talking about the kind that holds back water, though those are cool too. In the context of holiday lighting, dikes are a type of wire cutter or diagonal pliers that are essential for any serious DIY decorator. These handy tools are perfect for snipping through wires, zip ties, and other materials you need to manage when you're setting up your holiday light extravaganza.

Dimmable: The ability of a light bulb, string, or decorative lighting product to be dimmed using the product's dimmer or external dimming control. Non-dimmable indicates that they won't respond to a dimming switch and are not suited for displays that flash; this will damage them almost immediately in most cases. Some specialty bulbs that flash or twinkle might be dimmable but will usually have an undesired visual effect. Dimmability typically is only a question for LED lights, as incandescent bulbs and strings are universally dimmable.

Diode: Specific to light emitting diode (LED) lights, commonly referred to as "LED," is a small device designed to emit light using a very small amount of electricity. Some LED bulbs have more than one diode.

Drops: In the dazzling world of Christmas icicle lights, "drops" refer to the individual strands of lights that hang down from the main horizontal support wire, creating that iconic icicle effect.

– E –

Electrical Load: Electrical load refers to the amount of electrical power required by all the devices you've plugged into your circuit. Imagine your home's electrical system is like a buffet, and each device is a guest with an appetite. Some guests, like that big-screen TV or your smart refrigerator, are gluttons for power and pile their plates high. Others, like a humble nightlight, just nibble a bit. If too many power-hungry guests show up to the buffet at once, you can overload the circuit—hello, blown fuses and tripped GFCI (see "GFCI")! When planning your epic holiday light display, it's essential to know your electrical load so you don't fry your circuits and end up decorating in the dark.

End to End: In the world of Christmas lights, an end-to-end light set has a male plug on one end and a female plug on the other. This design allows you to connect multiple sets together, creating a seamless, dazzling display. Be aware that there is always a maximum number of strings that can be connected end-to-end. Check with the manufacturer to make sure you know the limitations. For incandescent light strings, this is particularly important since you may only be able to use a couple of them in an end-to-end configuration. LED strings are far more forgiving, usually allowing dozens of strings to be configured end-to-end. The number of strings that can be assembled in an end-to-end configuration is dependent on a variety of factors, including the gauge of the wire, the limitations of the fuse built into the male plugs, and others.

– F –

Faceted: An LED bulb style that uses a diamond-shaped gem cut pattern that allows light to reflect from multiple angles.

Flicker: The flashing that is visually perceptible in LED lights that are not adequately rectified (see "rectified"). The waveform of AC electricity causes the LEDs to turn off and on very quickly as the electrical current changes direction back and forth, causing a visible flicker in non-rectified LED lights.

Full Wave Rectified: see "Rectified/Rectifier"

Fuse: This tiny yet mighty component often sits in the male plug end of your light string, acting like a knight with a shield. It's there to protect your entire holiday spectacle by breaking the circuit if things start overheating. Fuses are there to stop electrical overload from turning your Winter Wonderland into a fiery fiasco. They're basically the bodyguards ensuring your lights twinkle safely.

Fused Plugs: Most string lights contain a fuse within the male plug end, which acts as a safety feature to prevent string lights from being overloaded with electricity.

– G –

GFCI Outlet: Ground Fault Circuit Interrupter (GCFI) outlets are essential for outdoor lighting as they protect against electrical shock and are required by electrical code for outdoor installations. Their job is to monitor the flow of electricity. If a GCFI detects an anomaly, it will stop the flow of electricity.

Guy Wire: A guy wire is a piece of wire attached to large and/or heavy decorations and usually runs at a 45-degree angle down to a ground anchor. One guy wire by itself isn't much help. They are always used three or four at a time to secure large, tall, and heavy decorations in place in case Mother Nature decides to try and wreak havoc on your display. They keep people and property safe when the wind gets out of control. To be effective, a guy wire should be attached to a ground anchor secured deep enough into the earth so that it will not come out even under hurricane wind conditions. The required depth will differ depending on the type of soil in your location. It is common for professionals to use vortex-style ground anchors between about 18 inches and 36 inches. You will need to use a depth appropriate for your soil type.

– I –

Icicle Lights: Icicle lights are designed to mimic the appearance of hanging icicles, typically used for roof lines and window frames.

Incandescent Lights: These are the OG Christmas lights, the ones that have been making our holidays twinkly long before LEDs joined the party. Inside each glass bulb, there's a tiny filament that heats up and emits a warm, golden light when electricity passes through it. Incandescent lights are known for being extravagant energy hogs and tend to have a shorter lifespan compared to their LED cousins. But hey, they bring that classic holiday glow that just screams, "It's Christmas!"

Inline Plugs: Inline plugs are the unsung heroes of the Christmas light universe. These handy little devices are situated partway along a string of lights, allowing you to branch off with another set of lights or plug in additional holiday decorations without having to run an extension cord all the way back to the main outlet. Think of them as magical portals that extend your decorating reach, letting you light up every corner of your festive wonderland.

Intermediate: In the realm of Christmas light aficionados, "intermediate" refers to an E17 socket size and bulb base size, most commonly linked to C9 Christmas light bulbs. Picture a socket that's playing Goldilocks—it's not too small like the E12 candelabra base, but not as large as the E26 bases you'd find on regular household bulbs.

– J –

Jumper: A jumper in the world of Christmas light installation is an indispensable tool for those aiming for a flawless and professional-looking setup, especially along rooflines. Essentially, a jumper is a length of bulk SPT (see "SPT/SPT1/SPT2") wire used to bridge gaps between sections of lights, ensuring continuous illumination without interruptions. It allows you to seamlessly connect different strands without leaving dark spots. Jumpers are particularly useful when there's a need to cover spans from one roofline to another, like over a porch or dormer, where you don't necessarily want lights to hang.

– K –

Kelvin: The unit of measurement used to describe the hue of a specific light source, basically telling you whether the light will make your space look like a cozy fireside or a surgical suite. Lower Kelvin values, like 2700 K, emit a warm, yellowish glow perfect for creating that inviting holiday atmosphere. Meanwhile, higher values, like 5000 K and higher, are more on the cool end of the spectrum—great for when you want to add an ice castle vibe to your winter wonderland. See "Color Temperature." **NOTE**: Different manufacturers often use different tolerances for kelvin ranges. So, one manufacturer may define 'warm white' as 2600-2900 kelvin, while another may define 'warm white' as 2800-3200 kelvin. This means that just because the label says "2800 kelvin," doesn't mean the color will exactly match a different manufacturer's "2800 kelvin." And even from the same manufacturer, the color can slightly vary from one manufacturing batch to the next. If you want consistent color, the best chance is to always order from the same manufacturer/source.

– L –

Lead/Lead Wire: The beginning of a string light from the male plug to the first bulb. For string lights, it is usually equal to the spacing between the bulbs on the string. For example, a string of lights with the bulbs spaced 6 inches apart will typically have a 6-inch lead and a 6-inch tail (see "Tail/Tail Wire"). For decor items such as LED rope light snowflakes, there will usually only be a male plug and the lead length will vary from a few inches to several feet.

LED Lights: LED lights are the modern marvels of holiday illumination! These tiny, yet mighty, Light Emitting Diodes have taken the Christmas lighting game to a whole new level. Not only are they more energy-efficient—dramatically reducing that post-holiday electric bill shock—but they also boast an impressive lifespan that could outlast even the most stubborn Christmas fruitcake. Available in a dazzling array of colors and configurations, LED lights allow you to transform your home into anything from a whimsical candy land to a sleek, high-tech winter wonderland. Plus, they stay cool to the touch, so you can deck the halls without worrying about turning your outdoor trees into kindling.

Lumens: Lumens are to light what horsepower is to cars. It's all about the oomph factor—the total amount of visible light emitted by a source. The higher the lumens, the brighter your lights will be. Don't worry too much about this term. It's not commonly used in Christmas light circles. Most folks prefer to use wattage as the relative gauge of brightness.

Lens - A decorative covering usually made from glass or plastic that fits over a light source to create the finished light bulb.

– M –

Max Light Strings End-to-End: There is a limit to the number of light strings you can use in an end-to-end configuration before things get dicey. This limit is like the max capacity of a roller coaster; you don't want to push it unless you fancy a thrilling, albeit fiery, Christmas display. Most manufacturers will specify this limit in the product specifications, usually somewhere around 3-5 strings for incandescent lights and quite a few more, often dozens, for their LED counterparts. Exceed this number, and you're flirting with an overloaded circuit, which could trip your breaker or even melt your wires. So, stick to the guidelines and spread out the holiday magic safely.

Medium Base Bulb: Also known as the E26 socket, this is the everyday hero of the lightbulb world and the same size socket you'd find in most of your household lamps and fixtures. When it comes to Christmas lights, medium-base bulbs are rarely used. But you may find them on some commercial and specialty bulbs.

– N –

Net Lights: Net lights are like a cheat code for hassle-free holiday decorating. Imagine a rectangular grid filled with lights, almost like a blanket, designed to be draped over bushes, shrubs, or small trees. Instead of meticulously wrapping individual string lights around every branch and inevitably missing spots or ending up with tangled messes, you just throw these bad boys on, and—boom—instant festive glory! Net lights give you an evenly-spaced, perfectly distributed glow with minimal effort.

– O –

Opaque: Sometimes also called "milky," this is a style of bulb lens that looks like old-school painted bulbs. Instead of seeing the tiny filament or LED inside, you get a solid, usually color-rich glow that's perfect for creating a vintage feel. Think classic, old-school Christmas bulbs that look like they've been plucked straight from a 1950s holiday postcard. These lights give your festive decor a nostalgic, retro vibe.

– P –

Polarized: A polarized male plug has one prong that's wider than the other. This design ensures that electricity flows in the correct direction, minimizing the risk of electrical shock. When you look at the female counterpart, you'll notice one slot is larger than the other to accommodate the polarized prong.

Pole Tree: A common Christmas tree design used in light shows and displays that uses a center pole with light strings hung from the top of the pole down to a wider ring on or near the ground. This creates a cone/tree shape made of lights.

Prelamped/Pre-lamped: This typically refers to a C7 or C9 bulb and stringer (see "Stringer/Socket Wire/Light Line") that come either pre-installed or hard-wired into a string light set. Economy-style pre-lamped strings will usually have hard-wired (i.e., non-removable) bulbs, while commercial/pro-grade pre-lamped strings will usually have screw-in (removable) bulbs.

Prop: In the world of Christmas decorations, the term "prop" is often used to describe a thematic element of your display. Think of props as the supporting actors in your festive production—characters that add depth, whimsy, and dimension to your display. Whether it's a larger-than-life inflatable Santa that waves at passersby, a family of lit-up reindeer grazing on your lawn, or a snowflake hanging on your home's facade, props bring your display to life. They're the pieces that turn your yard from "nice lights" into a "winter wonderland extravaganza," giving onlookers something to marvel at (and kids something to be utterly enchanted by).

– R –

Rectified/Rectifier: As related to LED Christmas lights. Alternating Current (AC) electricity likes to flip-flop between positive and negative, sort of like a light switch being flicked on and off really, really quickly. This can make your LEDs flicker, and not in a good, festive way. Enter the rectifier: This bad boy converts AC electricity into a steady Direct Current (DC), ensuring your lights stay gloriously bright and flicker-free.

Retrofit Bulb: This term was used a lot when LED bulbs first hit the market, since LED bulbs were often used to replace (or retrofit) the bulbs in existing incandescent light strings. These days, a retrofit bulb is just a C7 or C9 LED bulb. But you will still see the term used from time to time.

RGB: Stands for Red, Green, and Blue. These are the primary colors of light, and when you mix them in various combinations, you can create just about any color under the sun or, more accurately, 16,777,216 different colors! In the context of LED Christmas lights, RGB technology allows each bulb or string to change colors independently through a mix of these three hues. This means your Christmas display can be a dazzling, dynamic extravaganza of colors, shifting from serene blues and greens to fiery reds and purples at the touch of a button. Think of it as giving your Christmas lights a PhD in festivity. In most cases, RGB lights, also known as pixels, require a lot more technical wizardry than I will cover in this book, but there are some consumer-friendly, easy-to-use options out there.

Ridge Clips: A specialty type of C7/C9 light clip that allows you to install C7 or C9 light strings along the ridge lines of your roof without penetrating your shingles.

– S –

Series Wired: Series wiring typically uses a 3-wire harness, and the strings are designed to be constant current. That's electrician speak for "they like things to stay balanced." But here's the kicker: You can't just snip and trim these bad boys to fit the exact length you need. Nope, it's an all-or-nothing deal. They cannot be cut to fit. This is in contrast to 2-wire systems commonly used by C7 and C9 socket wires, which are more forgiving and *do* allow you to cut and splice them however you see fit in order to give your display a professional, custom-finished look.

SPT/SPT1/SPT2: SPT stands for "Stranded, Parallel, Thermoplastic," which I know sounds like something you'd need a doctorate in electrical engineering to understand. It's basically the rating for the insulation on your Christmas light wires. Here's the deal: SPT1 and SPT2 are the most common you'll come across. SPT1 has thinner insulation of 0.03 inches, which is fine for most household displays. SPT2, on the other hand, has thicker insulation of 0.045 inches, making it the beefier cousin that's better suited for harsher climates or longer-term installation. Think of SPT1 as the regular hot cocoa and SPT2 as the deluxe version with extra marshmallows—both are great, but one is just a bit more robust for when you really need it.

Stackable Plug: Stackable plugs feature a male connector on one side and a female connector on the other, allowing you to plug multiple light strings together (i.e., on top of each other) without needing more sockets. You will be surprised at how often this comes in handy!

String Lights: Available in various lengths, colors, and styles (more on these options in a later chapter)—everything from classic white to multicolored madness, string lights are the most common type of light used in Christmas decorating. You can drape them around your tree, hang them from your roof, or even wrap them around your cat - that's a joke, please don't sic PETA on me. Whether indoors or outdoors, string lights are the ultimate in versatile holiday cheer.

Stringer/Socket Wire/Light Line: A stringer is essentially the backbone of your C7 or C9 lighting setup. It's the electrical wire that comes adorned with sockets to hold your bulbs, be they C7, C9, or other types. Think of it as the garland upon which your festive hopes are strung, quite literally. The wire comes in various lengths and can be either pre-lamped (bulbs included) or ready for you to screw in your choice of bulbs. It's flexible and customizable.

Strobe Light/5mm Strobe Lights/C9 Strobe Light: Strobe lights are your secret weapon. Strobe lights are those flashy, blink-like-you-mean-it lights that create dramatic pulses of light. In the realm of Christmas lighting, they often come in compact sizes like 5mm or bigger, bolder forms like the C9 bulbs. They mimic the effect you'd get at a rock concert or a 90s dance club—short, intense bursts of light that can make your yard look like Santa's personal disco. Ideal for highlighting key features of your display or adding that extra "wow" factor, strobe lights take festive lighting to a whole new level.

– T –

Tail/Tail Wire: The end of a string light from the last bulb to the female plug. For string lights, it is usually equal to the spacing between the bulbs on the string. For example, a string of lights with the bulbs spaced 6 inches apart will typically have a 6-inch lead (see "Lead/Lead Wire") and a 6-inch tail. For decor items such as LED rope light snowflakes, there will usually only be a male plug, and the lead length will vary from a few inches to several feet.

Timer: A timer allows you to set specific on and off times for your Christmas lights, automating the entire process and saving you a heap of hassle. You can schedule your lights to turn on and off at times and intervals of your choosing. There are a few different types available, from manual timers (e.g., pin timers) to photocell timers to fully programmable timers, and I'll talk more about them later in this book.

Triple Dipped: This term refers to incandescent bulbs (see "Incandescent Lights") that have been coated in paint not once, not twice, but—you guessed it—three times. This triple-layering process results in colors that are rich, vibrant, and long-lasting.

Twinkle Lights: Twinkle lights are those little charmers that blink on and off at irregular intervals, creating a magical, ever-changing display. Think of them as the prima donnas of your holiday light setup, always vying for attention with their playful flashing. They can be fast or slow, subtle or bold, depending on the light set or bulb. Whether you want to mimic the serene flicker of stars in the night sky or give off a playful, energetic vibe, twinkle lights are your go-to for adding that extra sprinkle of whimsy to your festive decor.

– U –

UL Listed: UL stands for Underwriters Laboratories, a super boring name for a group that basically makes sure your Christmas lights won't turn your living room into a bonfire. When a product is UL-listed, it means that it has passed a series of rigorous safety tests and meets all the required safety standards set by these lab coat-wearing pros. In other words, it's their seal of approval that says, "Yes, this won't blow up your house."

UL Recognized Components: Being UL Recognized is a bit like getting a nod of approval from a very meticulous aunt who checks everything twice. When a component is UL Recognized, it's not the whole product that's been tested, but rather the individual parts. Think of it like a car; if the wheels, engine, and brakes each have their own little gold star from Underwriters Laboratories, they're UL Recognized. This means each component meets strict safety standards, even if the whole car hasn't been given the once-over by UL. Essentially, it's a thumbs-up that the parts themselves won't pull any shenanigans, even if they're part of something bigger.

– V –

Vampire Plug/Slide-on Plug/Gilbert Plug: Ah, the bogey monsters of the Christmas lighting world—vampire plugs! They have a unique way of sinking their "teeth" into your setup. Also known as slide-on plugs or Gilbert plugs, they are available in male, female, female inline, and splice versions. They are most commonly used for adding plug ends to your custom-cut C7 and C9 stringers (see "Stringers/Socket Wire/Light Line") and for adding male and female plug ends to your custom-cut extension cords (using bulk SPT wire!). **Note**: When using vampire plugs, be sure to use the same plug type as the insulation rating of your wire (typically STP1 or SPT2).

Voltage Tester/ Multimeter: This handy gadget is like the Swiss Army knife of electrical tools—it can measure voltage, current, and resistance and sometimes even double up as a continuity tester. Think of it as your electrical Sherlock Holmes, helping you solve the mystery of why your lights aren't twinkling or which part of your setup is acting like a Grinch. Whether you're troubleshooting a pesky circuit or just want to show off your nerdy prowess, a multimeter is the quintessential tool that brings serious problem-solving flair to your Christmas lighting game. For beginners, I recommend skipping the multimeter and picking up a product called "Kill-A-Watt" instead. It is much easier to use and understand. I'll talk more about it in the next section of this book.

Volts: This is the measurement of electrical potential, or in simpler terms, the "oomph" behind your Christmas lights. It's what pushes the electricity through the wires and makes all those pretty bulbs light up and dazzle your neighbors. For your standard holiday lights, you're typically looking at 120 volts in the US because that's the typical household voltage. Think of volts as the horsepower in your festive light display engine. Too few and you'll get a sad, dim display; too many and you could end up with a Clark W. Griswold situation—cue the explosion, but alas, no Christie Brinkley. So, it's crucial to pick lights and decorations that are compatible with your voltage supply to keep things merry and bright without any unexpected fireworks.

– W –

Watts (Wattage): Wattage measures how much energy your favorite festive bulbs are guzzling. Lower wattage equals better energy efficiency, meaning you can go full Griswold without needing your own power plant. For those who might have skipped physics class, it's all about how much juice each light bulb slurps up. There is some correlation here to brightness as well. Think about your household light bulbs; a 100-watt bulb will be much brighter than a 25-watt bulb, but it will also use a lot more energy. In other words, watts = power.

Wide Angle Lens: When it comes to 5mm LED Christmas lights, a wide-angle lens, also called conical, is the magic trick behind those stunning, evenly distributed glows. It is the Christmas light equivalent of a fish-eye lens on a camera – it spreads the light out over a broader area, ensuring that each LED shines its heart out.

Wire Gauge: Wire gauge is the measure of the thickness of both solid and stranded wire, and it comes with a quirky twist: the smaller the gauge number, the beefier the wire. It's like golf, where the lower score number is better. For instance, 22 AWG (American Wire Gauge) is a dainty little wire compared to the heftier 18 AWG. Why does this matter? Well, the thicker the wire, the more current it can handle without turning into a super-heated Christmas catastrophe. This is an important term to know when shopping for your Christmas light strings. Many economy light strings will skimp on both rectification (see "Rectifier/Rectification") and wire gauge by often using 24 gauge wire. Professional-grade light strings will most commonly be manufactured with 20 or 22-gauge wire. C7 and C9 stringers (see "Stringers/Socket Wire/Light Line") most commonly use 18 gauge wire, while permanent patio and bistro lighting will commonly use 16 gauge wire.

With these terms in your vocabulary, you are better equipped to tackle your Christmas light decorating projects with confidence and creativity. If you run into a term you don't know that isn't listed here, and you can't find it with a quick Google search, feel free to shoot me an email on our website at www.iam.christmas.

Your Toolkit

Essential Tools for Every Design

These are the basics you'll need, no matter what dazzling display you're planning to install—be it big, small, or completely out-of-this-world. Consider these tools the foundations of your Christmas lighting toolkit, whether you're a seasoned pro or just getting started.

Dikes/Cutters: Also known as diagonal cutting pliers, these handy tools are perfect for cutting wires, splitting wire prior to installing a slide-on plug, and more. They're also great for cutting zip ties, which we'll get to in a minute. With a good pair of dikes, you'll be able to tackle any wiring issue that comes your way.

Timer: This little gadget can be a lifesaver when it comes to managing your energy usage and keeping your lights on a schedule. Plus, who wants to go outside in the cold to turn off their lights every night? Note that most timers come with 1 or 2 outlets. Use multiple timers plugged into different exterior outlets if you need more than this for your display.

Types of Timers:

- **Manual Timers:** These are the most basic of timers; you simply plug your lights into them and manually set the on/off times using a dial or switch.

- **Digital Timers:** These are more advanced than manual timers, as they allow for more precise scheduling and often have additional features

- **Smart Timers:** These high-tech gadgets connect to your phone and allow for remote control of your lights, as well as more advanced scheduling options and smart home integration.

- **Photocell Timers:** These timers use a light sensor to automatically turn on your lights at dusk and off at dawn, making them perfect for outdoor displays. Just make sure you place the sensor in an area that gets enough light during the day.

- **Programmable Timers:** These timers allow you to set different schedules for each day of the week, making them great for those who like to mix it up with their lighting displays.

- **Advanced Timers and Control:** If you want to get really fancy with our display, try using something like the GFade 8 controller available at thechristmaslightemporium.com. The GFade allows you to not only schedule your lights to turn on and off in whatever way you want them to - including different times for every day or even multiple different times every day, but it also allows you to program the lights to turn on with a ramp up/fade, along with lots of other cool tricks. It will pretty much allow you to do anything you want with your lights.

Staple Gun and Staples: These are essential for attaching your lights to tree trunks and other surfaces that a clip just won't work. I recommend what is commonly known as a wire or cable stapler. These have a small notch/gap in the center that allows you to more accurately aim the staple without piercing a wire. Piercing a wire with a staple will usually cause a short and make your GFCI circuit trip - and becomes a frustrating undertaking to track down. So, be very careful not to pierce a wire with a staple. Double-check every staple you shoot to make sure it has not pierced a wire, and your life will be a much happier one.

Pliers: For those pesky vampire plug caps that are sometimes hard to slide-on or any other wiring needs, a good pair of pliers will come in handy.

Zip Ties/Wire Ties: Zip ties are a lifesaver when it comes to organizing your wires and keeping them in place. Use them to secure your light strands to trees and bushes, or to bundle up excess wire. They're also great for attaching chase controllers to frames, light strings to tree frames, and having about 100 million or more other uses. Zip ties are an indisputable, indispensable tool for decorators.

Pocket Knife/Blade: A pocket knife is a must-have tool for any DIY project, including installing Christmas lights. Use it to strip wires, cut rope, and remove those annoying white tags from LED Christmas light strings. Trust me, removing those tags will make your installation look tons better! It's also great for opening that pesky plastic blister pack packaging that seems to come with everything these days. Just make sure to keep the knife away from the kids!

Extension Cords: Extension cords are a must-have tool for any outdoor decorating project. After all, you have to get electricity from your power source to locations all over your front yard! Make sure to choose cords rated for outdoor use long enough to reach your desired location or use SPT wire and vampire plugs to make your own custom-fit cords for your display. Not only does this provide you with a super clean-looking finished project, but they are typically lighter weight and take up less storage room than store-bought premade extension cords.

Vampire/Slide-On Plugs: These plugs are essential for DIY decorators. They allow you to create custom-sized extension cords that fit perfectly with your display, saving you money and reducing clutter. They are also required to add plug ends to your custom-cut C7 and C9 stringers. Make sure you purchase the type of plug (SPT1 or SPT2) that matches the insulation rating of your wire.

Bulk SPT Wire: If you're planning on making custom extension cords or cutting your own C7 and C9 wire for a more professional look, bulk SPT wire is a must-have. The most common insulation rating for commercial stringers is SPT1, but you will also find SPT2. Don't forget to use vampire plugs that match the insulation rating of your wire to create perfect-fit extensions! Trust me, this will save you time and headaches!

Accessories That May Come in Handy

These items might not be on your "must-have" list if your design doesn't scream for them. But let's be real: Who doesn't want to make life a tad easier? You'll thank me later. Tedious tasks? A thing of the past. Your final product? Polished to perfection. You're Batman, and these are your trusty gadgets. Sure, you could fight crime without them, but why would you want to?

Christmas Light Clips: Although staples are great for holding light strings in place on a tree trunk or light-duty assembly of display props, they are a terrible choice for attaching lights to your roof, gutters, fascia, fences, brick, or just about any other surface. Gone are the days of using nails or staples to hang your Christmas lights on your house and other architectural features. Christmas light clips are a game-changer when it comes to holiday decorating. They're easy to use and won't damage your roof or siding. They come in a variety of sizes and styles to fit any type of light strand and for attaching lights to any type of structure.

- *All-In-One Clips/All Application Clips:* These universal clips can attach to gutters, shingles, and even tile roofs. They accommodate C7, C9, and light strings.

- *Shingle Tabs:* These clips are designed to hold screw-in C7 or C9 bulbs in a pointing-out position by sliding the 'tab' of the clip underneath the edge of a roof shingle.

- *Gutter Hooks:* As the name suggests, these hooks attach directly to the edge of your gutter, making it easy to hang icicle lights or string lights.

- *Brick Clips:* These clips are perfect for hanging lights and decor on brick surfaces. They clip onto the lip of a brick without causing any damage.

- *Tuff Clips:* These extremely popular clips are designed to hold C7 or C9 screw-in bulbs in an outward-pointing position when slid under a roof tile or in an upward-facing position when clipped to the edge of a gutter. They are made of flexible, extremely durable plastic that lasts for years, even in climates with a lot of sun exposure. These are the first choice of many professional Christmas light installers.

- *C-Clips:* This is a specialty clip designed for installing C7 or C9 screw-in bulbs along wood surfaces or any surface that you can drill a screw into. They are attached using screws. They are commonly used for installing lights along wood fences and deck railings.

- *Mini Clips:* These little wonders look a bit timid, but if you want to string icicle lights or standard string lights along a gutter, they will save the day!

- *Magnetic Clips:* These are perfect for attaching C7 or C9 lights to metal surfaces like a mailbox, a metal gate, or even a roof line with a magnetic surface. Just attach the clip, and you're good to go! No drilling or permanent attachment is required. Just be sure to purchase a magnetic clip compatible with your wire insulation (SPT1 or SPTT2) and the size of the light/socket you are installing - C7 or C9.

- *Lawn Stakes:* Lawn stakes are a requirement for outlining walkways, driveways, pathways, and flower beds with C7 or C9 screw-in bulbs to create smooth, straight lines and curves that look professional. Typically, they comprise a sturdy plastic stake with a round, flat surface on the top and lips on opposing sides to hold your bulb and wire in place.

Rubber Mallet: It might not be the first thing that comes to mind when you think "Christmas lights," but don't underestimate its usefulness! Imagine this: You've got a bunch of lawn stakes that need to be driven into the ground to hold light strings and display props. Using a regular hammer? Say hello to broken stakes and a whole lot of frustration. But with a rubber mallet, you can pound away carefully without worrying about shattering plastic or bending those stakes. It's also perfect for gently nudging yard decorations into place without leaving behind unsightly dents or scratches. It also comes in handy if you suddenly find yourself in a "Three Stooges" movie.

Hammer: If your display uses many heavy-duty ground stakes, such as rebar stakes holding guy wire for tall props, having a hammer handy will save you a lot of grief. For other, lighter-duty, and delicate uses like driving in plastic or aluminum stakes, consider a rubber mallet instead.

Hot Glue Gun: A hot glue gun can be a lifesaver when it comes to securing lights and decorations. Use it to attach light strings to frames or secure decorations in place. Just make sure not to use hot glue on delicate surfaces, as it can cause damage.

Drill With Driver and Drill Bits: You never know what having a drill with driver bits and drill bits at your disposal may come in handy. For example, if you are using C-Clips to attach C7 or C9 lights along a wood fence, you'd need to screw each clip to your wood fence. That's a lot of hand-twisting with a manual screwdriver! Go for a drill with a driver bit instead.

Work Belt: A work belt may not seem like an essential tool for installing Christmas lights, but trust me, it makes a huge difference. With a work belt, you can keep all your tools within reach and avoid constantly climbing up and down the ladder. Plus, the best use is as a holster for a stash of male and female plugs and their slide-on caps! I personally like to keep male plugs in one pocket, female plugs in another pocket, and slide-on caps in a third. Even a simple one will do. You'll wonder how you ever decorated without a work belt.

Ladder: This one is pretty self-explanatory. Unless you have a whole team of Santa's elves at your disposal to hang lights on your roof, you'll need a trusty ladder (or two) for those high-up places. Just be sure to follow the manufacturer's warnings and recommendations and read through the section on ladder safety in the next chapter.

Extension Pole: These handy installation poles allow you to install Christmas lights in hard-to-reach places without having to use a ladder. It is an extension pole with a specialized head on the end designed for hanging Christmas lights at heights. This can be a great help if you don't want to use a ladder, are afraid of heights, or don't have a lot of decorating to do on a high roof line or tall tree canopies. They are available in extendable lengths, usually up to about 24 feet. I recommend having one on hand for stringing lights around the outside of medium-size or smaller tree canopies and similar types of decorating projects.

Wagon/Utility Cart: If you have a large display or are working with heavy decorations, a wagon or utility cart can save your back from lifting and carrying everything. The 36th trip to the garage is not nearly as fun as the first trip.

Safety Gloves: Wear safety gloves to protect your hands while working with sharp edges or rough surfaces. Most folks are surprised at how easily a string of lights can cut their hands if you aren't careful or protected!

Kill-A-Watt: I recommend this product/device for quickly and easily measuring the electrical load of your display. Do a quick search on Amazon to find out more. It's much easier for a novice to use and understand than a multimeter/voltage tester (see "Multimeter"). It can even help you predict the cost of running your display for the Christmas season. It is an indispensable tool that every decorator should own.

With the right tools, installing your outdoor Christmas display can be fun and stress-free. From cutters to zip ties, make sure you have these essential tools before you start installing your masterpiece - and remember, the most important tool of all is your imagination (see Chapter 7). Remember always to stay safe while creating your ultimate Christmas masterpiece.

Chapter Four

Traditional vs. Modern Decorating

The Great Debate: Old School Charm vs. Techno-Wizardry

Let's kick things off with a showdown for the ages: the cozy, heartwarming nostalgia of traditional Christmas decorating going head-to-head with the jaw-dropping spectacle of modern, tech-savvy, synchronized music and multimedia light shows. It's like comparing your favorite old-school holiday specials with a high-octane Christmas blockbuster—both have their charm, but man, are they worlds apart.

Imagine sipping hot cocoa by a crackling fire, reminiscing about the good ol' days when all you needed were some twinkling lights and a bit of tinsel. Now contrast that with your neighbor's high-tech extravaganza that could give the Vegas Strip a run for its money. Each has its own charm, but let's face it—they couldn't be more different if they tried. It's like comparing apples to... well, space rockets.

Traditional Christmas Decorating: Charming and Timeless

Ah, traditional Christmas decorations—think of them as the ultimate comfort food of holiday displays, like your grandma's Christmas pudding that you secretly love more than the presents. These decorations are all about stirring up those warm, fuzzy yuletide memories of yore. It's a recipe that never fails, filled with:

Evergreens Galore: Think pine wreaths, garlands, and mistletoe, giving your space a natural, festive vibe—whether indoors or out.

String Lights: Classic twinklers in warm white or multi-colored, radiating that nostalgic glow we all secretly love.

Roof Outlines: The legendary warm white lights outlining your roof—a neighborhood favorite. If you only decorate one thing this Christmas, let it be this. Picture driving through suburbia in December, every house glowing with that same cozy white light. It's practically a suburban rite of passage and sometimes the only thing the sticklers on the HOA board are willing to let you do.

Homemade Ornaments: Crafted with love, these gems range from popcorn garlands to paper snowflakes. Each one tells a tale, and let's be real—nothing screams "holiday spirit" more than ornaments older than your kids.

Santa Claus and Reindeer Displays: Remember those kitschy ones your grandparents had on their lawn? Yep, red noses and all. There was a guy a few blocks over who put his on the roof. It fooled me roughly 35 million times, into believing that Santa was actually at his house.

Nativity Scenes: These simple displays are for those who like to keep it real and remind everyone of the season's true meaning. They bring a touch of heart and humility amidst all the sparkle.

Snowflakes, Penguins, and Snowmen: Perfect for those of you basking in balmy weather, where a rope-light snowflake might be your only chance at winter magic. There's nothing like a classic winter scene to spread joy. Plus, if you're the type who leaves decorations up until January, and by January, I mean March, this one's a winner that is less likely to spark the ire of an HOA than Santa and his reindeer!

A traditional approach to your outdoor Christmas decorating adds a snug, heartwarming feel to your holiday setup—perfect for rookies or anyone craving a nostalgic holiday throwback. It's not only about dazzling the neighbors but also keeping a piece of holiday history alive. So, break out the eggnog, crank up the carols, and make this year's outdoor Christmas decorating a festive trip down Memory Lane!

Modern Decorating: From Unique Color Palettes to a Symphony of Light and Sound

Modern Christmas decorating takes holiday cheer to innovative new heights with vibrant, eye-catching color palettes and symphonies of light and sound. Gone are the days when green, red, and gold were your only options. Today's yuletide creations embrace hues like teal, pink, purple, and even shades of neon to make your home stand out. These exciting new choices not only add a fresh twist to tradition but also allow for personal expression and creativity.

Neon Winter Wonderland: Picture vibrant blues, purples, and pinks mingled with cool white lighting. It's like the universe decided to throw a dance party in your front yard. Who needs a snowman when you've got this level of icy coolness?

Pastel Paradise: Imagine soft pinks, greens, and teals creating a whimsical, almost fairytale-like atmosphere. It's like your decor decided to take a magical, charming nap in a field of cotton candy clouds.

Monochrome Magic: Going all out with a single, unique color like pink gives you that sleek, modern aesthetic that screams, "I've got style, and I'm not afraid to show it."

RGB (Red, Green, Blue): Basic RGB strings are like mood rings for your house, slowly fading between blue, teal, lime green, and all the colors of a unicorn's rainbow mane. If you're a little tech-savvy, the more advanced RGB strings let you micromanage every bulb with 16.7 million color options. Yep, you read that right. Some even have your lights dancing in festive patterns like they're auditioning for a Christmas rave.

Rainbow Bright: Go full spectrum with bright, dazzling colors to create a space so lively it might just start singing. Picture your roof outlined with bulbs in all the rainbow's glory—red, orange, yellow, green, blue, and purple—making your house the envy of even the jolliest elf.

ColorSplash: Here's where it gets really fun—The Christmas Light Emporium (and yes, that certainly is a shameless plug) offers light strings and bulbs with unique palettes. With names like Havana, Stardust, Arctic, Holly, Cotton Candy, and Taffy, you're either buying incredible lights or some really innovative CBD. You can do a product search for "ColorSplash" at thechristmaslightemporium.com, and explore the most unique color palettes available.

These modern color schemes take your grandma's holiday decor and give it a funky twist, creating a festive vibe that's as fresh as a peppermint latte in July. It's like decking the halls with a splash of contemporary cool and blending the season's spirit with a pinch of pizzazz. Who knew tradition could look this good?

"What About Those Big Flashy Synchronized Music and Light Shows I See on YouTube?"

Now, stepping into the ring is the modern maestro—technology-based synchronized music and multimedia light shows. Think of it as the Christmas equivalent of a rock concert—the more lights, the better. HELLLLOOOO CLEVELAND, ARE YOU READY TO ROCK?

NOTE: *Synchronized light shows are definitely not for the faint of heart or the uninitiated. These are serious undertakings that involve all-year planning and weeks of installation of high-tech wizardry. Let's not even get started on the budget. It's probably best to tell your spouse the final cost on December 26. Even a modest synchronized light show with custom programming will cost you as much as a decent used car – and yes, I'm aware of that oxymoron. Most extravagant displays? It's either this or one of those trips into low orbit with Richard Branson. So, this is the only place in this book where we'll discuss them. They're cool if that's your thing. I've spent most of my career designing and installing synchronized light shows for everyone from Cesar Millan to the Atlanta Braves. But that's not what this book is about. This book is about the basics, helping you get started and helping you turn your dreams into neighborhood joy.*

>>>>> **PRO TIP** <<<<<

All of the principles I share in this book will apply if you ever venture into the wild world of synchronized Christmas light shows. You will still have to learn everything I mention in this book—and more.

Modern synchronized light shows often involve:

Synchronized Music: Imagine lights that groove to the beat of classic carols or modern holiday hits. It's like your house just joined a flash mob. This is where every synchronized music and light show begins. Also, everyone is using Trans Siberian Orchestra and Mariah Carey. Break free. Throw some "Christmas in Hollis" by Run DMC in there now and again.

Specialized DMX Lighting and Effects: Snow machines, moving head beams, flame canons—you name it. Often called 'production lighting and effects' thanks to their concert and theatrical roots, these high-end, complex effects are now all the rage in synchronized light shows. Just pray that White Snake or Motley Crue isn't driving by when you turn them on, or they might get out and think they're performing tonight.

Interactive Displays: Picture Santa waving and belting out "Ho Ho Ho" as people stroll by or singing snowmen welcoming guests. Maybe your visitors can even pick the next jam for your light extravaganza. How about a touch screen outside that lets folks 'draw' in brilliant color all over the front of your house? Your home basically turns into a real-life holiday theme park, minus the $300 entry fee.

Projection Mapping: Transform your home into a canvas with vibrant images, videos, or animations projected right onto your exterior walls. Want lasers outlining your windows while Santa busts a move in your living room? You can do that with projection mapping—if you've got the time, money, and know-how.

Fireworks: Some folks like to add synchronized fireworks to their big light shows, especially on special occasions like New Year's Eve. But fair warning: It's dangerous. DON'T TRY THIS if you're not a pro!

Drone Shows: As of now, not many private individuals have jumped on the drone light show bandwagon, but there are a few trailblazers out there. If you search the term on YOUTUBE, make sure you aren't at work, or you'll be down the rabbit hole for the next two hours on the company's dime.

Complex Networking: These high-tech synchronized light shows are no joke and require some serious tech skills. Imagine trying to connect controllers, lights, and music into one big, complex technology fruitcake—that's the reality if you want anything to work at all. If you're still having trouble getting your smartphone and your printer on the same wireless network, this might be one to skip.

Custom Software and Programming: The real magic behind these shows lies in the programming. Specialized software helps create lighting sequences that sync perfectly with specific songs or music tracks. It's like choreographing a dance—only for your lights. It's also extremely time-consuming, but if one of your strengths is attention to detail, welcome to heaven.

High-Tech Hardware: From RGB pixel and DMX controllers to advanced light strings of all magnificent types, these displays require some serious gear. Most of the time, you've got to build or assemble it yourself. DIY is the name of the game when it comes to synchronized light shows.

So, while synchronized light shows may not be for everyone, they definitely add a whole new level of excitement and spectacle to holiday decorating. This is the realm for your inner tech geek to shine brightly - pun absolutely intended. It's less about subtlety and more about making sure your display is the talk of the town—or maybe even the Internet.

>>>>> **PRO TIP** <<<<<

If you think you might be interested in exploring the world of synchronized music and light shows, start early. Give yourself at least a full year to learn the ropes. It's a lot.

Here are some resources you can look into if you think a synchronized Christmas light show might be in your future:

Decorating Groups

There are countless online and real-life groups where folks love helping newbies get the hang of things. Many of them are super into synchronized light shows. You'll also stumble upon a rich history of what's often called a "Mini." Local Christmas decorators all over the United States use this quirky term to describe their in-person gatherings. It's got a backstory that might surprise you.

Once upon a time, there was a single epic group – PlanetChristmas. Chuck Smith, its mastermind, kicked it off as an online forum for Christmas light enthusiasts to geek out together. It quickly snowballed into an annual trade show extravaganza every summer in Gatlinburg, Tennessee. PlanetChristmas was a right of passage for us old-timers. Eventually, some crafty local decorators spun off their own "chapters," dubbing themselves "minis" – like the bite-sized version of the big PlanetChristmas bash.

Today, PlanetChristmas is still an online forum full of important information you should digest and members willing to help out a newbie. The PlanetChristmas trade show is now known as Christmas Expo and is a traveling show geared toward 'extreme decorators,' popping up in a different American city each summer. Meanwhile, those "mini" groups are scattered all over the country like festive confetti. If you're looking to dive into the holiday decorating world – whether you're old-school or a high-tech wizard – these local minis are a fantastic place to start and show off your skills! Chances are, there's a group just around the corner, ready to welcome you with open arms and a few twinkling lights.

Here are a few examples of groups and shows for decorators. This list is by no means complete, far from it. I'm not endorsed by nor do I endorse any of these groups or companies; they are just the first few that come to mind, and that will make a great place to start your quest for light show glory. There are hundreds of decorator groups all over the country. Ask around, and you'll find one near you!

- **Christmas Expo**
  christmasexpo.com

- **PlanetChristmas**
  planetchristmas.com

- **Transworld's Christmas Show**
  transworldchristmasshow.com

- **Florida MegaMini**
  floridamegamini.com

- **Pacific NW CLAP**
  nwclap.com

- **So Cal Mini**
  socalholiday.lighting

- **North Texas Holiday Light-O-Holics**
  ntxhlworkshop.com

Synchronized Light Show Hardware and Software Resources

Hardware Manufacturers

Experience Lights is a manufacturer of RGB pixel controllers and related systems and RGB light show accessories known for innovative and feature-rich designs: experiencelights.com

Light-O-Rama manufactures AC and RGB light control systems and light show sequencing software. The first commercial provider to offer fully assembled, ready-to-run, and fully integrated light show control hardware and software: lightorama.com

Suppliers of Light Show Props and Accessories

Mattos Designs is a manufacturer and supplier of props, accessories, RGB lights, components, and decor; everything you could possibly need to bring your holiday vision to life mattosdesigns.com

Boscoyo Studios is a manufacturer of corrugated plastic props and accessories for RGB light shows: boscoyostudios.com

Light Show Programming Software

xLights is a free and open-source program that enables you to design, create, and play amazing lighting displays through the use of DMX controllers, E1.31 Ethernet controllers, and more: xlights.org

Light-O-Rama is a manufacturer of light show hardware and software. The Light-O-Rama Show Time Sequencing Suite is the premier commercially supported sequencing software used for creating synchronized light shows: lightorama.com

Service Providers

Extreme Lightscapes is a design/install company that works on projects all over the world. If your vision is extreme and you are looking to pay someone else to do all the heavy lifting, these guys have you covered. Disclaimer: I was the founder of Extreme Lightscapes, and I know the current owners very well. I endorse them fully. There are other similar service providers in the United States, but only some (like maybe 1 or 2) have as much experience as Extreme Lightscapes. www.extremelightscapes.com

A Blend of Both Words, Traditional AND Modern - or Somewhere in Between

Honestly, it comes down to personal preference. Do you want to wrap your holidays in the cozy, traditional warmth that feels like a giant Christmas hug, or are you looking to dazzle and delight with modern wizardry that's straight out of a holiday spectacular? There's no wrong answer. It's your display, your choice.

Some holiday heroes blend the best of both worlds, starting with traditional elements and sprinkling in a bit of modern flair. The result is a uniquely personal display that's both heartwarming and impressive. This can be achieved by using some of the less technical options available from places like thechristmaslighte mporium.com.

Chase Controllers—Add plug-and-play motion to your Christmas lights. This is the simplest way to add motion to your display.

Advanced Chase Controllers—These typically have more output channels and more built-in lighting effects to choose from. They are great for making a tree of lights spin around in circles and achieving other slightly more complex motions while keeping things plug-and-play.

GFade Controllers—The GFade controller is the world's most advanced chase controller. It is fully programmable and has a built-in timer and scheduling calendar. It requires no external software, as all the software is built in and accessible through a standard web browser. You can literally create any type of motion that your egg nog infused mind might conjure up.

Twinkle Lights—Talk about plug-and-play! Twinkle light strings can add just a touch or motion to your display, giving it just a little extra POP!

Strobe Lights—Speaking of POP! Strobe light strings, also known as Super-Spark strings, can add what looks like a million tiny camera flashes to your display—making your yard look just like the Rockefeller Center Christmas tree or the Eiffel Tower at Christmas!

Slow-Fade DreamSpark Lights—Just the opposite of strobe lights, DreamSpark strings have LED bulbs that very slowly and randomly fade in and out, bringing an elegant look to any interior or outdoor space. Some people say they look a bit like fireflies on an acid trip. Where these people acquired knowledge of how fireflies would respond if they were dropping acid is anyone's guess.

One thing's for sure: Whichever route you choose, your decorations will bring joy and spread holiday cheer because, after all, that's what it's all about. Now, go forth and decorate—whether you're a nostalgic traditionalist or a cutting-edge Christmas light DJ. Let the holiday cheer and your neighbors' unending envy begin!

Chapter Five

Electrical Basics and Safety

How Electricity Works

Understanding how electricity works requires a grasp of several key concepts:

1. Voltage

2. Current

3. Resistance

Voltage, often likened to the pressure pushing water through a hose, is the force that drives electrical charges through a conductor. Measured in volts (V), it's what propels the electrons from one point to another.

Current, measured in amperes (I), is the actual flow of electrons through the conductor, akin to the amount of water flowing through that same hose.

Resistance, measured in ohms (R), is the opposition to the flow of electrons, much like a narrowing in the hose that restricts water flow. Ohm's Law connects these three basic principles with a simple equation: Voltage (V) = Current (I) x Resistance (R).

All electrical systems, from the simplest flashlight to the most complex computer, operate based on the interaction between voltage, current, and resistance. Understanding these basics is crucial for anyone delving into electrical work or troubleshooting issues with electrical systems – including Christmas lights and light-up decor.

Understanding Polarity

The polarity of electrical flow is an essential concept that ensures the proper functioning of electrical devices and systems. At its core, polarity refers to the direction of the electric current.

When dealing with direct current (DC) systems, polarity determines which direction electrons flow, typically from the negative terminal to the positive terminal of a power source. Correct polarity ensures that electrical devices like LEDs, batteries, and motors operate as intended. For instance, connecting a battery with reversed polarity can damage the device, potentially leading to short circuits or irreversible harm. I believe this is also how The Matrix comes online.

In alternating current (AC) systems, while the current flows back and forth, understanding the hot and neutral connections is still crucial for safety and device performance. Bad wiring can not only cause equipment failure but can also pose significant safety hazards, including the risk of electric shock or fire.

But why is polarity so important? Mix up the positive and negative ends, and you might fry circuits faster than a short-order cook flipping burgers. It's all about making sure those little electrons know where to go and what to do, making your gadgets work like a charm instead of creating unintended pyrotechnics. So, remember: When it comes to electricity, polarity isn't just a nifty term—it's a key player in keeping everything running smoothly and safely.

Electrical Safety

We've all heard the saying, "Safety first!" Well, when it comes to electricity, nothing could be more true. While playing with little electrons is a core requirement for the successful installation of your Christmas lights, it's important to handle and use electricity with caution. Here are a few basic safety tips to keep in mind:

- Always turn off power sources before working on any electrical device or circuit.

- Use protective gear like gloves, goggles, and insulated tools when dealing with electricity.

- Keep liquids away from electrical devices and outlets, and never touch them with wet hands.

- Make sure cords and wires are not frayed or damaged before plugging them in.

- Never overload outlets or extension cords with too many devices plugged in at once.

- If a piece of your decor, light string, etc., has a grounded male plug on it, always use a grounded extension cord to run power to it. Don't remove the ground pin! It's there for a reason!

While these may seem like common sense reminders, it's always good to go back to basics and prioritize safety when dealing with electricity. After all, the last thing you want is for your hair to stand on end like a mad scientist's experiment gone wrong, right? So, keep these tips in mind and stay safe while enjoying the wonders of electricity!

Using a Basic Multimeter to Measure Volts and Amps

A multimeter is an essential tool for anyone working with electrical systems, allowing you to measure voltage, current (amperage), and resistance with ease. Here's a step-by-step guide on how to use a basic multimeter to measure volts and amps:

Measuring Voltage (Volts):

1. **Prepare the Multimeter:** Turn the multimeter dial to the voltage measurement (V) setting. If measuring DC voltage, make sure the dial

is set to "DCV" or the "V" with a straight line and dashed line. For AC voltage, set it to "ACV" or the "V" symbol with a wavy line.

2. **Insert the Probes:** Plug the black probe into the COM terminal (common) and the red probe into the VÙ terminal.

3. **Connect the Probes:** Place the black probe on the ground or negative terminal and the red probe on the positive terminal of the circuit or component you wish to measure.

4. **Read the Measurement:** The multimeter display will show the voltage present in the circuit. Ensure the reading is within the expected range for your specific application.

Measuring Current (Amps):

1. **Prepare the Multimeter:** Turn the dial to the current measurement setting (A). Be mindful of whether you are measuring DC - symbolized by a straight line and dashed line - or AC, which is symbolized by a wavy line, current.

2. **Insert the Probes:** Plug the black probe into the COM terminal. For measuring lower currents, plug the red probe into the mA (milliamps) terminal. For higher currents, plug the red probe into the 10A terminal. Ensure your multimeter can handle the expected current without exceeding its rating.

3. **Break the Circuit:** Unlike voltage, measuring current requires you to insert the multimeter probes in series with the circuit. Disconnect the circuit where you want to measure the current and connect the probes, ensuring the current flows through the multimeter.

4. **Read the Measurement:** The multimeter display will show the current

flowing through the circuit. Take the necessary precautions to avoid exceeding the multimeter's amperage rating.

Safety Tips:

- Always start with the highest current or voltage range and then adjust downward to prevent damaging the multimeter.

- Double-check your connections before taking a measurement to avoid short circuits.

- Be aware of the multimeter's limits and only use it within its specified ranges.

Using a multimeter correctly can help diagnose and troubleshoot electrical issues efficiently, assuring both the functionality and safety of your electrical projects.

>>>>> **PRO TIP** <<<<<

Use a "Kill A Watt" Device to Measure Amps and Voltage. It's much easier and safer to use than a multimeter. You can find them on Amazon and other online shops. I recommend it for new decorators and anyone who just wants a simpler, safer, easier way to measure and manage the power behind your magnificent Christmas display.

Voltage Drop: *Understanding Voltage Drop Over Distance When Using Long Extension Cords or Installing Long Runs of Lights*

Voltage drop is a critical factor to consider when using long extension cords or long runs of lights, especially in scenarios where maintaining consistent electrical performance is essential. Voltage drop refers to the reduction in voltage in an electrical circuit between the power source and the load end due to the resistance of the extension cord conductors. The longer the extension cord, the greater the resistance, which can lead to a significant voltage drop.

You can often tell when you have a voltage drop problem because the lights closer to the end of your long run will be dimmer than the lights at the beginning of your run.

The amount of voltage drop depends on several factors, including the length of the cord, the gauge of the wire, and the amount of current being drawn by your lights. Thicker wires have less resistance and therefore, experience less voltage drop over distance. Conversely, thinner wires (higher gauge numbers) will have greater resistance and more pronounced voltage drops.

To minimize voltage drop over distance, use shorter extension cords whenever possible, choose cords with thicker wires, and ensure that the current draw is within the extension cord's rated capacity. Being mindful of these factors will help maintain electrical efficiency and make sure your lights light up brightly all the way down your long string.

How to Avoid Electrical Fires and Other Dangerous Situations

Several factors can cause electrical fires when installing your Christmas lights.

One common issue is using lights with frayed or damaged wires, which can create arcing. Electrical arcing occurs when an electric current flows through the air between two conductors or within a damaged cable instead of following its intended path. This can happen when wires are frayed or exposed, causing electricity to jump from one point to another. Arcing produces intense heat, which can ignite surrounding materials and lead to an electrical fire. It also poses a risk of electrical shock and can damage your lights. To prevent electrical arcing, it is essential to regularly inspect your holiday lights for any signs of wear and tear, ensuring that all cables and connections are intact and securely insulated.

Overloading electrical outlets or extension cords by plugging in too many lights or decorations is another significant risk, as this puts excessive strain on the electrical system and can lead to overheating, melting of your extension cords, and fire.

Additionally, using indoor-only rated lights outdoors without proper protection from the elements can result in water exposure, short circuits, and electricity leakage that creates a safety hazard.

Take These Critical Steps to Avoid Fire Hazards:

- Always use lights and extension cords rated for the intended use, and never exceed 80% of the extension cords' rated amperage capacity.

- Check for any wear and tear on your light strings, decor, and extension cords.

- Avoid the use of nails and staples whenever possible - they can pierce wires, causing exposure to moisture, tripped circuits, and even arcing/fire hazards.

>>>>> **PRO TIP** <<<<<

NEVER plug a coiled electrical product directly into a power source without unrolling it and cutting off the length you need! Coiled bulk wire products like SPT1, rope light, etc., will create high levels of resistance if left coiled AND plugged into a power source. This can lead to melting and fire. Trust me. I've seen it happen more than once.

Making Your Own Extension Cords and Bulb Stringers

Making Your Own Custom Extension Cords

As Christmas decorating enthusiasts have grown in number over the years, their displays have become larger and more complicated. One of the early complications and expenses of designing and building a large Christmas display used to be extension cords. Extension cords are not only expensive but also can create a very large and often ugly mess of tangled wires that distracts from the beauty of the display. However, with some careful planning, you can shave some costs and clean up those piles of extension cords by building your own custom-fit extension cords using SPT1 lamp cord and SPT1 slide-on vampire plugs.

Slide-on plugs are often used by professional Christmas light installers. They allow you to make your cords custom fit the lengths you need and provide a more organized, cleaner, professional result. This is especially helpful if you design and install a large Christmas light show. You can very quickly find yourself with hundreds or even thousands of extension cords to manage.

Here's how to clean up the mess by making your own extension cords using SPT1 wire and SPT1 slide-on vampire plugs:

These instructions apply for both the male slide-on vampire plugs and the female slide-on vampire plugs, as well as inline female plugs and slide-on couplers

1. Determine the length of SPT1 lamp cord you will need for each run.

2. Cut the SPT1 wire to length, but do not strip the insulation from the wire.

3. If your SPT1 slide-on vampire plugs already have the slider backs on them (this is unusual), remove the slider back. If your SPT1 slide-on

vampire plugs and slider backs are already separated, move on to the next step.

4. Slightly split the end of the wire that your plug will be installed on by either snipping it down the center about 1/16"-1/8" or simply pulling it apart with your fingers.

5. Insert the SPT1 lamp cord into the small pocket at the enclosed end of the plug. The pocket will have a small divider in the bottom center. This is why you made the small split in the previous step - so that the neutral and hot sides of the exposed wire end are separated when installed into the pocket. *This is very important. If you don't split and separate the end of the wire, it will leave the exposed wire susceptible to arcing and fire hazard.*

6. Make sure the end of the SPT1 lamp cord goes down into the pocket and fits nicely. Be sure the ribbed side of the SPT1 wire is on the right-hand side so that the polarity is correct. The ribbed side of the SPT1 lamp cord needs to contact the large plug tip. Once the SPT1 lamp cord is properly inserted into the pocket, bend the SPT1 wire so that it makes contact with the two sharp points (vampire teeth).

7. Now simply slide the cover onto the plug. The cover is designed to press the SPT1 lamp cord into the sharp points (vampire teeth) as you close it, thereby making the electrical connection.

Making Custom Socket Stringers for C7 or C9 Bulbs

Have you ever needed a light string for your blow mold that has just one socket or wanted a string of C9 sockets for hanging strobe lights at 24-inch spacing? These are examples of the two most common reasons you might want to know how to make a custom stringer for your C7 or C9 bulbs.

By using SPT1 wire and C7 or C9 replacement sockets, you can make a C7 or C9 stringer with a custom number of sockets or custom spacing between sockets or both!

C7 and C9 replacement sockets work in a way similar to slide-on plugs. When you buy them, they will come with a socket and a small cap that snaps into the bottom of the socket after you run your wire through it. When you push the bottom cap onto the socket, the pressure of putting the bottom cap on will force the wire down onto the neutral and positive pins that supply power to the socket.

>>>>> **PRO TIP** <<<<<

The best tool to push the bottom cap onto a C7 or C9 replacement socket is a vise grip C-Clamp. These have flat plates that swivel, allowing them to lock the bottom cap in place evenly and quickly with much less effort than trying to push the bottom cap on with your bare hands.

Moisture Protection

There are quite a few accessories available that will help you make your display as moisture-resistant as possible. These include:

Gasket seals for grounded and ungrounded extension cords. There are a couple of solutions on the market that will help keep your connections between extension cords and between end-to-end light strings as moisture-free as possible. These include the Twist and Seal line of products that are available at most big box stores and the extension cord gasket and cover solutions that are available at places like The Christmas Light Emporium. The gaskets help seal connections between two connected extension cords, while the plugs can be inserted into any exposed female plug to help prevent moisture intrusion.

Socket seals for C7 and C9 bulb sockets with bulbs. This is one of the most popular moisture prevention items available. They are especially useful if you like to install your bulbs facing straight upward. With an upward-facing installation, the sockets are far more susceptible to water getting into them and causing corrosion and other issues. A socket seal gasket is installed along the rim of the socket, in between the socket and the bulb. When the bulb is screwed into the socket, the rubber seal forms a moisture-resistant barrier between the bulb and the socket.

Socket caps/covers for unused/open C7 and C9 sockets. Sometimes, you may end up with unused sockets (no bulb in the socket) on a stringer. The ***Socket Stuffer from The Christmas Light Emporium*** *are the best solution available for securing open/unused C7 or C9 sockets* - keeping them moisture-free and keeping curious fingers safe!

>>>>> **PRO TIP** <<<<<

Don't wrap your electrical connections with electrical tape. If you do, moisture created by condensation or leakage will likely get inside the connection. The only way to dry them out will be to remove the tape and let them dry out. It's also a pain if you have other troubleshooting issues to resolve, like needing to replace a light string that has been taped together with other strings in an end-to-end connection. Pro installers don't wrap electrical connections with electrical tape, and neither should you.

Ladder Safety and Working at Heights

Ladder Types

Extension Ladders: The top choice among Christmas light installers due to their versatility and ability to reach significant heights. These ladders consist of two or more sections that slide and lock into place, allowing users to adjust the height as needed. They are ideal for accessing rooftops, high windows, and tall trees, making them perfect for elaborate light displays.

A-Frame Ladders: A-frame ladders are self-supporting and typically consist of two sets of legs connected by a hinge at the top, forming the shape of the letter "A" when opened. These ladders are designed for stability and ease of use, making them ideal for reaching places where a support structure is not available.

Step Ladders: This is another popular option for hanging Christmas lights, especially for lower heights and indoor decorations. They are self-supporting and have a wide base, providing stability on flat surfaces. These ladders are easy to set up and move around, making them suitable for tasks that involve frequent repositioning, like reaching tree trunks and branches that are just a little out of reach.

Telescoping Ladders: Offer a compact and convenient solution for Christmas light installers. They collapse into a small, easily transportable size and extend to various heights, similar to extension ladders. These ladders are handy for installers who need to move between multiple locations and require a space-saving option.

Articulating Ladders: Also known as multi-position ladders, they are highly versatile and can be configured into different shapes, such as A-frame, extension, or scaffold. This adaptability makes them valuable for Christmas light installation on various surfaces and in challenging spots. Their ability to transform into different ladder types means fewer tools are needed to complete the job efficiently. But be aware that they are usually heavier than extension ladders.

General Ladder Safety Tips

When hanging Christmas lights on your home, following these ladder safety tips can help ensure a safe and enjoyable decorating experience:

Inspect the Ladder: Before use, thoroughly inspect the ladder for any signs of wear, damage, or defects. Check for loose rungs, missing rivets, and any instability that could compromise your safety.

Choose the Right Ladder: Select a ladder that is appropriate for the height and type of decor you will be installing. Ensure it can reach the areas you intend to decorate without overextending yourself.

Set Up Properly: Place the ladder on a stable, level surface. Avoid slippery or uneven ground, and if working on soft soil or turf, use ladder stabilizers or levelers to prevent sinking or tipping.

Angle the Ladder Correctly: When using an extension ladder, follow the 4:1 rule – for every 4 feet of ladder height, place the base 1 foot away from the wall. This angle enhances stability and reduces the risk of the ladder sliding out.

Secure the Ladder: If possible, have someone hold the base of the ladder while you climb. Additionally, secure the ladder at the top using ropes or ladder hooks to prevent shifting or slipping.

Maintain Three Points of Contact: Always maintain three points of contact with the ladder – two hands and one foot or two feet and one hand. This rule helps maintain stability and reduces the risk of falling.

Avoid Overreaching: Do not lean too far to the sides. Climb down and reposition the ladder if necessary rather than stretching to reach further.

Dress Appropriately: Wear sturdy, non-slip shoes to ensure a good grip on the ladder rungs. Avoid loose clothing that might get caught, and consider wearing gloves for better grip and protection.

Don't Overload the Ladder: Be mindful of the ladder's weight capacity and avoid carrying heavy decorations or tools while climbing. Instead, use a tool belt or have someone pass items to you.

Work During Safe Conditions: Avoid using ladders in inclement weather, such as high winds, rain, or snow. Ensure adequate daylight when decorating outdoors to maintain visibility and safety.

By adhering to these ladder safety tips, you can decorate your home confidently and create a beautiful, festive display for the holiday season.

>>>>>   **PRO TIP**   <<<<<

Pay attention to the maximum weight rating from your ladder manufacturer. This is important. I'm a big guy and I work with a lot of big guys. We need beefy ladders. You don't want your ladder collapsing while trying to spread your holiday cheer - or ever!

Helpful Tools and Accessories for Working on Ladders, On the Roof, and at Heights

Installing Christmas lights on a house's roof can be a daunting task, but having the right tools and accessories can make the job safer and more efficient. Here are some essential items that can assist you:

Cougar Paws (brand) Work Boots: Designed specifically for working on roofs, this is the choice of roofers and pro Christmas light installers. The boot soles are made of industrial Velcro. Called the "hook," it allows a replaceable "Peak Series" pad to be attached to the sole. One side of the Replaceable Pad, called the "loop," is made of felt material. When attached to the "hook," it holds firmly. When the pad wears down, it can be peeled off and replaced by a new one.

Pitch Hopper Roof Wedge: Made from super strong foam with a soft foam bottom, it grips roof shingles when downward pressure is applied, creating a flat surface or 'step' to help stabilize when standing or kneeling on a pitched roof.

The GOAT Step Assist: A patented climbing system for steep pitched roofs makes it easy to climb a roof with confidence. It looks like a long pole with handles every couple of feet and attached to your roof ridge, providing handles to hold for stability.

Ladder Stabilizers: These are devices that attach to the top of your ladder and extend for additional stability. They help keep the ladder steady and protect gutters and siding from damage, providing a flat surface against the house.

Tool Belt or Pouch: Keeping your hands free while on the ladder is crucial for safety. A tool belt or pouch can hold your clips, light strings, and other small tools, allowing you to easily access them without needing to climb up and down frequently.

Extension Pole: This can help you hang lights in hard-to-reach places without a ladder. They are particularly useful for attaching lights to eaves, tall trees, and the highest points around the perimeter of your house.

Roof Anchors and Harness: For those working on high or steep roofs, using a roof anchor and a safety harness can provide extra protection against falls. These safety devices can be lifesavers and are worth the investment.

Hard Hat: Nobody ever wants to wear the hard hat! But if you do happen to take a tumble, it just might save your life. Seriously.

Having these tools and accessories will not only enhance your safety but also make your Christmas light installation process more streamlined and enjoyable.

Avoid Common Injuries

Decorating your home with Christmas lights can be a joyous activity, but it's not without risks. Understanding common injuries and knowing how to prevent them is crucial for a safe decorating experience.

Falls from Ladders: One of the most common injuries is falling from a ladder. This can result in broken bones, sprains, or even head injuries. To avoid falls, always ensure your ladder is on a stable, level surface and follow the ladder safety tips mentioned earlier. Never overreach, and always maintain three points of contact with the ladder.

Electrocution: Dealing with electrical decorations can pose a risk of electrocution. This can happen if lights are faulty or if water comes into contact with electrical elements. To avoid this, inspect all lights and electrical decorations for any damage before use and ensure they are rated for outdoor use. Additionally, keep cords and light fixtures away from water sources and unplug lights before making any adjustments.

Cuts and Punctures: Handling hooks, staples, and other sharp objects can lead to cuts and puncture wounds. Wearing protective gloves can help safeguard your hands while handling these items. Use plastic clips whenever possible instead of metal staples, metal clips, screws, etc., to attach lights to your house, as plastic clips are safer and less likely to cause injury.

Strains and Sprains: Lifting heavy decorations or repeatedly climbing ladders can lead to muscle strains and sprains. To prevent these injuries, use proper lifting techniques and don't attempt to carry too much at once. Stretch beforehand to loosen muscles, and take breaks to avoid overexertion.

Eye Injuries: Installing lights can sometimes result in eye injuries from poking yourself with branches, decorations, wire, or even zip ties! Wearing safety goggles can protect your eyes from such incidents.

By being aware of these common injuries and taking preventive measures, you can reduce the risk and safely enjoy the process of decorating your home for the festive season. Remember, people DO die every year while installing Christmas lights! Don't be one of them!

Safety Notes: Children, Pets, and Critters

Ensuring your outdoor Christmas light display is safe for children, pets, and outdoor critters is essential to avoid accidents and injuries. Children sticking a finger in an open light bulb socket, pets urinating on light strings, and outdoor critters chewing on wires - these are common safety issues that can be avoided with a bit of planning. Here are some tips to help you maintain a safe and festive environment:

Use LED Lights: LED lights are cooler to the touch than traditional incandescent bulbs, reducing the risk of burns. They are also more energy-efficient and have a lower voltage, making them safer for children and animals.

Secure Cords and Wires: Ensure that all electrical cords and wires are securely fastened and not left dangling. Use appropriate clips to attach them to walls or fences, keeping them out of reach of curious children, pets, and wildlife.

Elevate Lights and Decorations: Place lights and decorations higher up, away from the ground. This makes them less accessible to pets and outdoor critters while providing a safer environment for children to play around.

Use Protective Covers: Invest in protective covers for your outdoor sockets and plugs. These covers can help prevent water damage and deter animals from nibbling on electrical components.

Eliminate Tripping Hazards: Keep walkways and play areas free of tangled wires and decorations. Use outdoor-rated extension cords designed to blend in with their surroundings or are specifically marked "trip-proof."

Supervise Children and Pets: Always supervise children and pets when they are near the decorated areas. Teaching children not to touch the lights or climb on decorations can also prevent accidents.

Avoid Harmful Chemicals: If you use any artificial snow sprays or chemical treatments on your lights or decorations, ensure they are non-toxic and safe for both children and animals.

Check for Damage Regularly: Regularly inspect your lights and electrical components for signs of wear and tear or damage from animals. Replace any damaged items promptly to maintain a safe display.

By following these guidelines, you can create a beautiful and safe Christmas light display that will be enjoyed by everyone, including your furry friends and the local wildlife. Happy decorating!

Chapter Six

Lighting Styles, Types, and Options

This is a learning book, first and foremost, but I'm going to tell the honest truth. When you walk into a store asking for Christmas lights, but you have no idea what kind you want - or maybe you don't even know that there's more than one style, shape, or type - the store employees know you're a rookie. That's by no means a bad thing because everybody has to start somewhere, but it's a big reason why you definitely need to keep this guide handy. When diving into the world of Christmas lights, prepare yourself for a wild ride. The sheer variety can make you feel like you've stumbled into the Jawa sandcrawler from "Star Wars." Seriously, who knew there were this many choices? It's like Christmas decided to throw a rave and invited every bulb in the galaxy. So, if you're scratching your head over names that sound like intergalactic party favors, you're not alone. In this chapter, I'm going to name the lights, along with their strengths (and weaknesses), to get you up to speed.

One note before we start any of it is that no matter what you settle on, make sure that your lights are rated for outdoor use. There are a lot of beautiful options out there that count on the comfort of the home and having a roof over their heads. If you use the wrong type, you're going to find yourself in the dark and swiftly out of money when the first raindrops or cold spell short-circuit all your hard work.

LED? Or Incandescent?

Let's start at the top of the list - with the battle between LED and Incandescent Christmas lights. Incandescent lights are usually going to be more affordable, and considering that some displays have thousands upon thousands of lights, that can be a very appealing choice to make. But they're cheaper for a reason. First of all, they consume more energy, which will bite you on the back end, especially if you want to be the person who leaves the lights on all night for those hardcore fans who swing by at 2 a.m. when the crowds have died down outside your epic display.

LED lights are going to cost more upfront, but that's because the quality is improved. They use less energy, they operate at a lower temperature, and they last longer - with some rated up to 100,000 hours - the equivalent of 4,167 days, or about 11-½ years. There are numerous types of LED bulb types to be aware of, including the 5MM conical, the G12, also known as the raspberry, the M5 mini light, and the C6, more commonly known as the strawberry. LED lights are also available in a lot more color options and motion styles than incandescent lights. For example, check out the SuperSpark, DreamSpark, and ColorSplash lines at The Christmas Light Emporium.

Beyond that big distinction, we can break our categories down even further.

Mini String Lights

A long-time favorite, these have small bulbs and are a timeless classic. This term is sometimes used interchangeably to reference LED strings (chiefly 5mm or M5 style LED strings due to their similarity in size and shape to traditional incandescent light strings) and traditional incandescent string lights. It is most commonly a reference to incandescent light strings.

LED Light Strings

There is a huge variety of shapes and styles of LED string lights available. But the most common are the four standard shapes and sizes of 5mm, M5, G12, and C6 – plus two larger bulb styles, C7 and C9, that are available in pre-lamped string form and also available as screw-in bulbs. The main difference between the various styles of LED string lights is the size and shape of the lens and how they disperse light.

When it comes to decking the halls with LED Christmas light strings, choosing the right style can feel like deciding whether to give a cat a bath—equally confusing and fraught with potential peril. Let's break it down:

5mm Light Strings

These little guys are the stealth ninjas of the Christmas light world. Small and bright, the 5mm LED lights pack a serious punch in terms of lumens per inch. They are also sometimes called "wide angle" or "concave" because of the small divot in the top of the lens that helps make these bad boys the single brightest point of light available in a Christmas light string. They're fantastic if you want to add a brilliant sparkle to your display without overwhelming the senses. Plus, their compact size means you can string 'em in tight spaces or even hide them in that shrubbery your landlord swears is "just a little overgrown." They are also easier to handle, install, take down, and store than some of the larger lens styles. Hence, this is the choice of most professional decorators.

M5 Light Strings

Similar to the 5mm but with a longer and faceted lens that resembles a traditional mini light string, M5 lights give off a slightly softer glow. They're like the friend who shows up to a party with snacks instead of drinks—a little more laid back. Some folks prefer M5 strings for decorating their Christmas tree because they are the LED string style that most closely resembles a traditional Christmas light string.

G12 Light Strings

G12 lights are the chubby little ornaments of the bunch. With a round shape, they create a delightfully vintage vibe. Perfect for those who want to evoke a sense of nostalgia and warm fuzzies.

C6 Light Strings

C6 lights are like the middle child of LED options—often overlooked but undoubtedly vital. They're shaped like little strawberries (and sometimes referred to as such), giving them a charming flair. The benefits? They're great for those who want something eye-catching but not overly flashy. It's another great choice for decorating your Christmas tree if you want a more traditional look.

LED C7 and C9 Light Strings (pre-lamped)

Not to be confused with C7 and C9 screw-in bulbs, C7/C9 pre-lamped LED strings are usually the same size as their screw-in bulb counterparts but have some essential differences. The bulbs are generally not removable, they are usually not as bright as their screw-in bulb cousins, and the bases are the same size as all other pre-lamp LED string styles, so they don't fit or work with standard Christmas light clips. I often call pre-lamped C7 and C9 LED strings "economy" style strings because they are much less expensive than their screw-in bulb version. While they make another excellent option for decorating your Christmas tree, some folks insist on using them to outline windows and rooflines. If you're on a budget, that's fine. But professional installers will never use pre-lamped C7 strings round windows or pre-lamped C9 strings along a roofline because they are impossible to install in a perfectly straight line, thereby losing that professionally installed look.

C7 and C9 Screw-in Bulbs

Available in various colors and lens finishes, these are the workhorses of outdoor Christmas decorating. They are commonly sold in sets of 25 individual bulbs that you screw into a matching stringer (a length of wire with sockets pre-installed down the line, a male plug on one end and a female plug on the other) that are purchased separately. The most popular lens finishes for these bulbs are the opaque lens – which looks a lot like the old-school painted bulbs, and the faceted lens – which offers a brighter dispersion of light and is the most popular modern option. At about 1.5 inches tall, C7 bulbs are commonly used for outlining doors and windows, and some people love them on their Christmas tree. At about 2.5 inches tall, C9 bulbs are widely used to outline rooflines. This is what you see in every neighborhood during the Christmas season – C9 bulbs outlining just about every roof you see lit up.

Net lights

These are a great catch-all when you need some shrubbery or foliage lit, and you don't want to go through the painstaking task of stringing them. You can gently 'throw' these lights like you're going crabbing over the vegetation in question and arrange it so it fits on snugly and completely. They usually come in a 4ft x 6ft size 'blanket,' so they don't work for every type of bush or shrub and sometimes take a little finagling to get them to fit your shrubs just right.

Icicle lights

These are the much safer version of the chunk of icy death that almost kills

Ralphie near the end of "A Christmas Story" when the movie-length prophecy that he'll shoot his eye out if he gets an air rifle for Christmas nearly comes true. They are usually reasonably short in length of about 7ft and available in LED 5mm or M5 styles and a wide variety of colors. You can also find them in versions that twinkle or even slow fade for a more magical look.

Floodlights vs. Spotlights

These might look the same on first blush, but they are far from it. The biggest differences are the angle of the beam and the width of it as well. Floodlights are designed to illuminate a large area. Say you've got the entire nativity scene going on, and you want to make sure everyone knows that the donkeys are in the barn, the wise men are making their way from the driveway, and the angel is on top of the manger; these are the way to go. They have a beam angle around 45 degrees and their beam of light is quite wide. By comparison, a spotlight has a lower angle (30 degrees) and casts a much narrower beam of light to focus on one solitary thing. To remember it better in your mind, the floodlights are when you're showing the whole chorus on the stage during the school assembly, while the spotlight is when you ignore all the brats and just focus on your precious angel in the front row. They are available in various sizes, styles, shapes, and colors.

>>>>> **PRO TIP** <<<<<

Use flood lights to add that 'pro' look to your outdoor trees. Even if you wrap your trees with light strings, adding the same color flood light pointing from the ground and up into your tree will add a massive touch of elegance and really make them pop! You can also skip wrapping a tree with string lights altogether and just use flood lights to light them up!

Rope light

Rope lights are a sturdier version of string lights, with the LED bulbs housed in a flexible, clear PVC tube. This is a great choice if you're going to try making your lights follow paths and create non-traditional shapes, such as signs, swirls, and other motifs.

Special Effects Lighting Used in Christmas Displays

You probably already know if you're the kind of person who isn't going to be happy with the same old, same old when it comes to Christmas lights. Like, when you see Santa on the roof in the sled, your immediate thought is - wouldn't it be great if you could see real puffs of smoke coming out of his pipe? Or if instead of reindeer, he had an F-16 engine underneath the slay, and every 30 minutes or so it belched out a giant fireball? Yeah, I see you. Real recognizes real. If you're aspiring for non-traditional lighting to stand out in the cul-de-sac, win the coveted "Best In" neighborhood award, or be picked up by a Russian spy satellite for your sheer energy output, here are a few terms to know:

Moving heads

Moving head beams are like a miniature version of those giant spot lights you used to see in the sky indicating "something BIG must be happening over there!" or the Bat Signal the city of Gotham shines into the sky when they need Batman to come to the rescue. They are all about intensity with a concentrated beam of light that can highlight different areas of your display and create dramatic effects. Not to be confused with the Talking Heads, who created "Burning Down the House" – these bad boys have a family tree that stems out of the production lighting world and are easily the most dramatic (and most expensive by a long shot) type of lighting that extreme decorators incorporate into their displays.

Strobe lights

Used by college kids doing drugs and bands in clubs, strobe lights are also great for simulating movement in your display. You can go with the traditional type or a string of them to add the effect over big parts of your display.

RGB lights

The acronym stands for red, green, and blue, which sounds pretty limiting until you realize you can create more than 16 million hues from those three primary colors, resulting in literally any shade of anything you might need. If you go this route, be sure you know what you're getting into. There are consumer-friendly RGB products available from the big box stores and online at The Christmas Light Emporium. But there are also extremely complex systems available that require all sorts of software and hardware to make them turn on, let alone change colors and create patterns.

Twinkle lights

Trendy in the suburbs where HOA restrictions limit the big displays that make the holidays so memorable; these are very beautiful in their own way, especially when the whole street or whole neighborhood is similarly adorned. Usually, every 4th or 5th bulb on the string blinks on and off at random intervals.

Chapter Seven

Decor Styles, Types, and Options

For decades, it was all about the lights and only the lights unless you happened to be extremely crafty and knew your way around a workbench and a power saw and understood lots and lots about art, light, perspective, and so forth. Most of the best displays you see are still 100% Do It Yourself, but the industry has absolutely blown up when it comes to extra large and unlit decorations – often called "daylight decor." You can plan these out quite a bit in advance because online stores like ours have their catalogs open year-round. I'm also pretty convinced that stores like Target and Home Depot keep their employees locked inside the stores on Halloween. Then, when the clock hits midnight on November 1, they put all the All Hallow's Eve decorations in the half-off bins and launch everything from the Christmas warehouse into those empty display cases. BAM! Instant Christmas!

Where do we start with daylight decor? Let's start simple and build it out.

Wreaths

If you trend towards the religious power of Christmas and the traditional feel of the holiday, one or more wreaths is a great way to show your faith. Wreaths have multiple meanings in the Christian face, including as a symbol for Jesus Christ's suffering and triumph over death, as well as the joy and victory that are tied to the Christmas spirit and the everlasting life associated with believing in God. Plus, they are the most traditional of all traditional decor!

Garland

Most decorators like their garland on the inside, which looks lovely adorning a mantle, a staircase, and any other linear display. Garland also represents eternal life via the intertwining of evergreen branches and victory over death. If you put garland outside, ensure it can withstand the stresses of the weather. Many garlands have unique adornments, like pinecones, fake "snow', and holly berries to augment the idea of Christmas. Garlands look great outlining your front door, too!

Wood cutouts

As mentioned in the lead, wood cutouts are a fantastic look back at the past of the decorating community, to a time when every dad had five saws in the garage and knew how to get any length of wood at any time of day or night. One of my favorite Texas neighborhood light efforts - Prestonwood, just outside of Houston, started its tradition with wooden cutouts all the way back in 1977 and is still a very popular destination for fans of the holiday. The wooden cutouts in multiple themes have passed from one set of homeowners to the next, and most of the original participants put in their sale agreements that anyone buying the home had to keep up with the tradition! Even if the neighbors don't want to pitch in, you can do these yourself or buy them online and have a decoration that will last for years, if not decades, with proper care.[1]

---

1. D-B, A. (2023). *Guide to Prestonwood Christmas Lights 2023 in Houston.* [online] HoustonOn-TheCheap. Available at: https://www.houstononthecheap.com/prestonwood-forest-christmas-light s-houston/ [Accessed 8 Aug. 2024].

Commercial 3D displays

You'll see these a lot at the front of subdivisions or in large office buildings, but there's nothing wrong with 'going big' for extra holiday cheer. Oversized nutcrackers, snowflakes, snow fairies, giant bows, candy cane lanes, 40-foot-tall Christmas trees - you name it, you can buy it and make it part of your yearly tradition. Just make sure you have enough space to store them safely and that your neighborhood doesn't have a problem with oversized objects that can be seen from the interstate.

Blow molds

If you're old enough to remember the good old days, then blow molds probably make you smile immensely when you see them in someone's yard. For the unfamiliar, these are hollow decorations that are created by a process of 'blowing' plastic into an existing mold cavity, largely resembling the art of glass blowing. The plastic is heated to expand, and once it cools, it can be transformed into a light-up decoration. Santa, reindeer, and snowmen have always been the go-to designs, along with the traditional nativity scenes. After dying out for a time, they've started to make a comeback in the 2020s, with sellers on Amazon and the like making kits available to do them yourselves and plenty of folks making a business out of refurbishing old blow molds and selling them to decorators everywhere!

Wireframe displays

Wireframe displays are a nice touch because you get a basic shape that allows the human imagination to fill in the details while you adorn it with lights that help with your overall theme. Reindeer are among the most popular forms these take. Since they are so lightweight, manufacturers will often add a small motor that lets them move their heads or some other part of the display back and forth to bring them to life – at least with wireframe displays that can be found at big box stores. But if you really want to get creative, there are companies (including The Christmas Light Emporium) that stock wireframe displays in a dizzying array of pre-designed themes – everything from snowmen and Santa to flowers, gnomes, candy canes, dolphins, and more. Plus, if you have a vision for something unique, many folks like us can take your design and fabricate a commercial-quality wire-frame display just for you!

Inflatables

It seems like there are two polarized camps when it comes to inflatables - you either love them and can't wait to see what's coming out next year, or you hate them and wish that you had a blowgun handy as you drive by to wipe them out one by one. I don't have a dog in the fight, but I understand the desire of some people to get into the holiday spirit with a decoration that they don't need to do more than attach to an extension cord to get it ready to go every night. They are reasonably quiet unless you have a whole bunch of them, and they are easy to secure and store if the weather gets nasty outside. The downside is that the already commercialized holiday gets even more so when you suddenly have a block full of Minions singing carols, Snoopy and Woodstock joining Santa on his sleigh, and Baby Yoda laying away in a manger with the Death Star overhead.

Chapter Eight

Choosing a Theme

Even writing that title made me cringe back to my freshman year of high school. My English teacher - whose name I will omit here for fear she might read this and come after me - drilled theme writing into our heads like a drill sergeant on a daily basis. If you don't have a theme, she told us, you wouldn't be making an A or a B. When we failed to heed her warning, the first few papers she returned would read, "No theme, C+" or "Where's the theme? C-". By the time she had reviewed 25 or 30 theme-less batches of babbling from a bunch of absent-minded 15-year-olds, the remaining papers would just say, "THEME? F".

On a side note, this same teacher, upon finding out it was my birthday, told me that my present was to go first on the day that we all had to stand up and recite a 40-line poem. Yeah, she was a sweetheart.

I might have yet to understand the purpose of a theme in high school, but I can tell you that it has immense value in your Christmas light display. I guarantee you that every street has at least one house where it's obvious that the folks decorating the yard have no idea what's going on and just bought everything they saw, started setting it up, and are even now inside by the surge protector praying to God that they don't blow a fuse and burn the whole city down. Some of these folks claim that organized chaos is their theme. They throw everything out there like the young version of me playing with an old Spin-Art toy from the 1980s where you sprayed different colors onto a piece of hard paper and whirled them around in a paint spinner, then pretend that what you had done constituted some form of art.

Themes are important for your display because the goal here is to put on a performance, a scene, or a work of art for the people passing by your home. You're the director, the producer, the costume designer, the special effects artist, and every other job you might find on a TV or movie set. Several years back, a news anchor, when doing a story about the opening night of my light show, referred to me as being "as nervous as a musical director on opening night." I was.

Themes let you tie together various elements to make one cohesive display that will immediately let people know what they're looking at - while enhancing their enjoyment of the display. Naming your theme will also help you improve it over time as you become more and more aware of what items, patterns, and colors could tie into it. Trust me when I say that once you have a theme and give it a name, you'll start seeing things everywhere that you think might be a good addition. Then, your only problem will be how much of your bank account gets eaten up in your production design!

There are literally hundreds of themes to choose from, but I'm going to hit on just a few here to give you some ideas and get your glitter-filled mind stirring. Don't worry about sticking strictly to any of these. You'll find over time that your theme will be unique to you as you add more and more years of effort to your light display.

Theme Examples

Traditional

There's no place like home for the holidays, and there's no more recognized theme for Christmas light displays than the traditional Christmas theme. This is the Christmas that most of us in the 20th century remember as the classic Christmas - the red, white, and green color spectrum - green trees and garlands, white snow on the crown, and red dominating the ribbons, the ornaments, and of course, the trim on the suit of a certain jolly old elf who brought us all the happiness in the world every December 25th.

Of course, the real tradition is the one that is the real reason for the season - the birth of Jesus Christ, the miracle that we celebrate with the nativity scene, resplendent with Mary, Joseph, the manger, the angles, the farm animals, and of course, Baby Jesus at the heart of it all. Nativity scenes aren't really big on garish displays; in fact, my favorite nativities are usually the simplest, with a simple spotlight or floodlight putting the focus on the obvious center of attention and everything else fading into the shadows. I'm happy to say that very few companies mess around with any inflatable or other 'modern' versions of the nativity scene; there's a certain understated elegance of white lights, wooden cutouts, and simple shapes. I love the look of white lights surrounding a manger and the nativity scene. While I have a reputation for being a big-time lights and display guy (i.e., a Christmas decorating snob), there are a whole lot of things I like about the simple stuff.

As powerful as our religious icons are during the Christmas season, it's hard to resist decorating your house and yard with the big guy that the kids go crazy for - of course, I'm talking about Kris Kringle, St. Nick, Santa Claus himself - the big man with the big belly, the bigger heart, and the ability to somehow hit every house in the world all in one night. Santa is always welcome in a traditional yard display, whether he's up on the rooftop (click, click, click), dangling precariously from your chimney, or decked out in full regalia in your front yard. It's hard to go wrong when it comes to Santa. I've seen him in Bermuda shorts and sunglasses, flying an airplane, riding on a fire truck, and kicking it with a beer in his hand on different occasions. Sometimes, I've even been the hardcore, dedicated type - dressed up as Santa and stood outside in my display as people came along, giving them an extra dose of Christmas cheer and a moment for the little ones to remember forever. If you have Santa, it's not uncommon to see his reindeer along for the ride. Rudolph is a popular choice, as his red nose is an easy win for even the most novice of light engineers. A red bulb - one with a simple flasher controller - often brings lots of extra attention - and you're good to go for the duration of the holidays.

If you want to go an extra step in the traditional realm, you can't go wrong by including scenes from everyone's favorite Christmas ballet - "The Nutcracker". Written by Pytor Tchaikovsky in 1892, it is one of the most beloved and per-formed Christmas media experiences the world over. It also gives us some of our most vivid imagery of the holiday season - the toy soldiers, the Nutcracker himself, the sugar plum fairy, and more. It's so well-known - most cities put on countless performances of it during the holiday season - that you could easily do a themed display that was solely the Nutcracker, and almost everyone would instantly know what it is.

Modern

I've had more than a few people tell me I need to get with the times over the years - mostly about the way I dress - but it hasn't done them much good. Modern Christmas light displays are another matter that I love seeing and working on, as they give you a chance to showcase your own spin on the Christmas celebration.

A big hit for a lot of people who go modern is the "mega-tree." A 'Christmas tree' shape is formed by draping lights from the top of a pole and down to the ground in a circle around the pole and forming the shape of a cone – a tree! - and usually with a star on top. Sometimes also animated with controllers to make it dance around. I also like the look of these giant spheres that a lot of people put in their yards; it's like an ornament fell off some huge Christmas tree somewhere and landed in your yard. They come in all kinds of color combinations, and you can always make your own using any style, shape, design, and color combination you want!

The lights can be one color or many colors or even colors that change or colors that "dance" to a musical soundtrack. The musical factor is a big contribution to a lot of modern light displays, involving an app or a piece of computer software to get everything synced up, as well as a short-wave radio transmitter to broadcast your choice of music for a limited distance. If you go this route, don't forget to put a lot of signage up for people driving by to be able to tune their radio to the right station, and make sure to hit that sign with a spotlight - it's not so easily seen in the dark when every house in the block also has light displays up. If you've seen more than a few of these displays, you probably know that the hard-pounding Christmas selections of groups like Mannheim Steamroller are super popular because they are so fast and frenetic that they draw a lot of attention to the house. That's definitely a well-traveled road to go, but if you're going through all the trouble of the unique lights and the combination of visual and audio, I have to say I'd love to see some Yuletide obscurity get put into the mix. At the top of my list is "Christmas in Hollis" by 1980s rap legends Run DMC - a great beat and something that is a far cry from the powerhouse strings and harps of everyone's favorite steamroller. Another option is to surprise people with a really passionate religious ensemble and perhaps have it all go dark at some point, except for a nativity scene. Selections like "Joy to the World," "Away in a

Manger," and "Silent Night" are known to everyone at this time of year but not always the most-requested songs on the jukebox.

If music isn't your thing, there are still tons of modern options out there to try and give a more contemporary look to your design. Alternate colored lights are a nice starting place. I really like the combination of blue and white together, as it reminds me of cold weather and chilly nights growing up. Using rope lights allows you to turn modern everyday items in your yard into artistic endeavors. Plenty of people have free-standing lamp posts in their yards. You can wrap rope light around it in red and white and make it look like the world's most yuletide barbershop pole of all time. But don't stop with the obvious. Giant planting pots, any other outdoor decor like statutes, or even garden gnomes can get dressed up for the holiday season if you're creative with how you decorate them. I'm also a fan of the oversized wreath for the modern look. It captures the classic feel of the potent power of God and Jesus at this time of year, but if you've got your yard decked out, nobody is going to notice that same old wreath on the door. So, jumbo size the wreath and find a more appropriate place to display it. If you have a two-story house, mounting it up high with an appropriate spotlight will really make it stand out as the centerpiece of a modern display.

In the suburbs and the city, you'll find a lot of hand-painted signs that local vendors go door-to-door, or social media to social media, to sell. Most are painted on wood and have a festive message like "Season Greetings from the (your name here) Family." Some will have an artist's rendition of the family or a cool Christmas original artwork or something that represents them. If you order one of these, make sure that the person selling it knows how to use punctuation properly. It might not bother everyone, but seeing these signs with bad apostrophe usage drives me up the wall every year. Driving around, I see the sign that says, "Happy Holidays from the Johnson's!" and, although I hate to be the grammar nerd, it's "the Johnsons" - plural, not possessive. If you don't notice it until after the fact, maybe sweet-talk the vendor for a minor touch-up so my freshman-year English teacher doesn't see it and demand that you stay after school on Monday!

As technology increases, you can do some really spectacular things with your Christmas decorations without the commiserate hundreds of hours of manpower. Some traditionalists avoid this route, thinking they need to be the Great Griswold, and at some point find themselves hanging upside down from a tree, praying to God that approaching vehicles don't run over any live wires and accidentally electrocute them. But that's not everyone. Technology is designed to make our lives easier, including getting the house looking good for Christmas and being as cool and exciting as you want it to be.

One way to go about this is with the Virtual Santa digital download that has become popular in recent years. You can use this very video effect to make Santa appear to be looking out the windows of different rooms of your house with multiple scenes and actions. It's a great eye-catcher, and if little kids come by your house, their minds will be blown for the rest of the season. You can combine it with a DVD player and use any rear projection material (even something as simple as a translucent shower curtain will work. Curtain sheers work great!) to show St. Nick walking around, checking his list, waving, eating the milk and cookies, and even checking his dreaded list not once, but twice.

Other technology that plays well in your decorations include projection lights, also known as laser light projectors. They use a combination of mirrors and lasers to project images and/or colorful lights onto any part of your house or yard. The rotating mirrors give the illusion of movement, and the light passes through a lens that displays a picture - how the Bat Signal worked for Commissioner Gordon in the comic books. These started out as just lights, but there have been all sorts of advancements as time goes on. One of my favorites is snowflakes falling down. It's beautiful to look at and will drive any visiting dogs absolutely crazy as they try to catch them.

Rustic

Almost everyone in the US lives in a big city these days, but about 60 million (17.9% of the population) still live in rural America. At one point or another, that was pretty much all of us. There's a natural feeling of hearth and home associated with Christmas on the farm or Christmas in the country that is vastly different from how we celebrate it in the city or the suburbs.[1]

The feeling of "going home for Christmas" definitely rings a lot truer in the rustic theme: the kids have gone off to live in the big city, join the military, or find their fame and fortune somewhere else. Driving down a dark country road to a house full of Christmas lights with a roaring fire and a festive Christmas tree seen through the front window on a snow-covered evening feels like you've stepped into a Norman Rockwell painting, and you're in no great hurry to leave!

When it comes to rustic Christmas displays, it seems like wood plays a major theme in the decor, and I'm talking about the hardiest of woods like oak and pine. Handcrafted signs, wooden cutouts of trees, reindeer and nativity scenes, and even miniature Christmas villages fit the bill. This is another great spot for using rope light. If you actually live somewhere rural, you can wrap it around the tractor, the farm tools, the fence posts of your barn or stable, or even turn your scarecrow against a Christmas Crow for a few nights. Wreaths with hardier stock, like crops and pine cones in them can be lit up to symbolize the flavor of the season and the joy of a good harvest.

When you talk about lights and colors for rustic displays, I'm a big fan of warm colors that light up the scene without dominating it. White lights are a wonderful look - it is telling your viewers that this is a special occasion, but the feeling of

---

1. America Counts Staff (2018). *What is Rural America?* [online] The United States Census Bureau. Available at: https://www.census.gov/library/stories/2017/08/rural-america.html.

home is the special part. An outdoor Christmas tree is always welcome in the rustic display; after all, being able to tend to the vegetation is the key to survival on every farm. Using lanterns for additional light outside is another nice touch. Another great area to unpack for outdoor decorations is to remember what it was like growing up on the farm when it came to being a kid. There was no Internet, no TV, and maybe an old transistor radio, but that's where the gadgets ended. That meant a lot of making your own fun, and when it snowed for weeks on end, there was no item more coveted than the sled. Whether you have one, buy one, or make one, the kind of sled that would provide endless hours of hilltop fun for the entire family is a must for the perfect rustic Christmas look.

If you're the type that likes to engage and interact with the people who come by your house to see your display, a really clever way to kill two birds with one stone is to put out some cozy chairs, a table, and lots of blankets for those cold winter nights. Do a little research on the peak times that people come by and make a big pot/pitcher of hot chocolate, bust out the marshmallows and the mugs, and invite anyone who happens by to park the car, sit a spell, and enjoy some homemade hospitality from you and yours. Whether it's the neighbors you've never talked to or people visiting from out of state, this is one of the best ways I've ever seen to spread some authentic holiday cheer without a shred of imperialism involved. In Texas, we call that 'being neighborly.'

Whimsical

Remember at the start of this chapter - we talked about the yard on every street where the people look like they just dumped everything from the garage and started plugging stuff in? That qualifies as whimsical because sometimes your theme is that there is no theme. Other times, the theme is something really out there that makes sense to you and maybe nobody else, but that's OK, too.

Whimsical means anything that you associate with Christmas or anything that you think would be fun for Christmas.

For some decorators, that means going all out with a Disney or Star Wars or Charlie Brown Christmas motif, with signs and music and big blowup decorations in the yard. I love them all. If you are passionate about a particular branded theme, why not celebrate it on the year's best holiday? I've also seen folks channel Christmas movies into an entire theme for their decorations. A house here in Texas goes all out on "A Christmas Story" every year, including a 20-foot tall model of the legendary leg lamp that the Old Man wins in a contest and displays proudly in his front window for the whole neighborhood to see. I don't have to tell you this piece of Christmas decor is an absolute show-stopper. In fact, the neighborhood HOA eventually moved it from the yard to a public spot on a cul-de-sac so it could be viewed from all angles and wouldn't cause god-awful traffic jams every night. I've also seen a fantastic display based on the most controversial Christmas movie of all time - "Die Hard." Why controversial? Despite the movie taking place at Christmas time and at a Christmas party, with John McLane trying to get home for Christmas, many people say it's not a Christmas movie because the film was released in late July. This display not only had a version of "Santa" in a chair with the light-up sign saying "Now I have a Machine Gun," but also an imitation of the vault from the end of the movie - rigged to open slightly with lights and playing the soundtrack's "Ode to Joy."

Movies and TV shows are great, but they are also just the tip of the proverbial iceberg when it comes to the full range of what a whimsical display might look like. You could emulate the Coca-Cola ad campaign and have your whole yard be polar bears celebrating the holiday - or some other animal you happen to love - like beagles, pigs, or hammerhead sharks (I mean, I guess that's possible). You can do Christmas in the future or Christmas on another planet or try to recreate your 5-year-old self's idea of what Christmas looked like to you.

You can pick a color and decide that every single thing in your yard is going to be some shade or hue of that color - even if it's not a Christmas color. In Texas, we have two giant colleges that are the fiercest of rivals, whose colors are about as opposite as anything on the color spectrum. The University of Texas Longhorns are all things burnt orange, while the Texas A&M Aggies are completely maroon. You'll find yards decked out in both colors - although never at the same time - throughout the state. Using your alma mater's colors or the colors of your favorite pro sports team, or dedicating your yard to Elvis Presley, Taylor Swift, or "Weird" Al Yankovic are all well within the endless boundaries of the whimsical theme.

The overarching point I'm trying to make about whimsical themes - and every other theme - is that you should absolutely let your imagination run wild. There is no wrong way to design a display, but I've seen plenty that push the envelope there. A more honest opinion is that there's no arguing taste or style, and whatever theme, design, or pattern makes you happy is the perfect one for you, and nobody (except maybe that pesky HOA board) has the right to tell you anything differently.

Where to find Inspiration

Starting from scratch and constructing a perfectly decorated yard for Christmas isn't exactly the easiest thing in the world. Sometimes, I watch those cake-baking competition shows where they all have to develop and execute a theme in just a few hours. One person on every team is somehow the best artist of all time and will sketch out this unbelievable drawing within a few minutes. Me? I think if you gave me 10 minutes, I could probably draw something that resembled a cake. Maybe. My point is that not everyone is an artist, an architect, an engineer, or Leonardo da Vinci when it comes to envisioning what you want your yard to look like. For that reason, just about everyone needs help finding inspiration for what they want their design to be.

The easiest place to start is with your own eyes and ears as you drive around your city and see the kind of things that catch your eye. If you have some neighborhoods that you know are chock full of good ideas, I'd suggest parking at the end of one street and walking the neighborhood with your smartphone, taking pictures of the displays you really like. You can come back in the daytime for a better look at what certain things look like if you need more clarification; don't go tromping on their property without permission, or you might get a rustic Christmas shotgun in your face.

If you don't see anything in person that blows your socks off, take a good gander at some of the more choice sites online. Although the massive PlanetChristmas forums have been on a sabbatical for a couple of years, the incredible community has found a new home on Facebook - join the fun and scope out what other passionate designers are up to at https://www.facebook.com/groups/planetchristmas.

You can also search the likes of TikTok, Instagram, and YouTube for great Christmas displays. Not only will you get a ton of inspiration, but you'll also be able to follow and eventually interact with some fantastic people who are incredibly passionate about this time of year and going all out for it. Many of them are not just decorators but also teachers of the craft and include step-by-step and how-to videos that can really help you out if you're looking to emulate something that you've seen them do.

If you're not all that familiar or comfortable with social media, another tremendous resource is Pinterest. The website will occasionally nag you to sign up, but you don't really have to. What you see here are people's pinned pages of all their favorite versions of pretty much anything under the sun. Christmas decorations are a super popular topic on Pinterest, and you can use keywords to narrow your search to get some great results. To prove my point, I typed in "outdoor rustic

Christmas" just now and have yet to reach the end of the list of different pins that people have posted - you will find it to be an almost limitless visual resource.

It also won't hurt to go to a big online Christmas store like **The Christmas Light Emporium (.com)** and start browsing or searching for what's out there, what sort of centerpiece item you might like, or to get a visual of all the things you're learning about here. Lots of decorators are a lot better at seeing something right in front of them than they are at trying to conjure it up in their minds, and some of the best ideas are ones that you see online that inspire you to put together something truly unique!

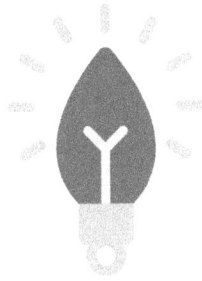

Chapter Nine

Planning Your Spectacle

Once you've decided on a theme and you've got an idea of how it might all come together, it's unfortunately time for my least favorite part of the Christmas season: The reality check.

It is time to estimate your Christmas decorating budget, calculate what you can afford, and determine how to get from Albuquerque to The North Pole without permanently going into debt or catching your significant other Googling "how to return 735,000 Christmas lights on December 26".

Big dreams are great. Shooting for the moon? You bet. If you want a fully-functional Santa-theme roller coaster that plays Scorpions "Rock Me Like a Hurricane" at 150 decibels every night, I certainly admire your ambition. And I want to see it when you get it installed!

Make a Budget and Stick to It

Like any 'love' project, we have to bridge the gap between what we want and what we can afford. When we have passion projects, especially tied to our homes, we tend to get a little sloppy about keeping things on budget.

- A new pool

- A family vacation

- That backyard shed that you told your wife you were turning into a man cave, but now it's more of a subterranean Fortress of Solitude and has more square footage than your actual house.

You get the idea. Coming up with a budget before you start pricing everything is probably the best idea because when you do it the other way around, you start rationalizing that there's not much difference between $500 and $700, then $700 and $900, then $900 and $9,000 (it's just an extra zero!)

Finding Discounts

The good news is that the budget on paper isn't the budget that you have to abide by. I'm not talking about stealing but finding ways to save money by being smart. The best thing you can do in this mindset is to start planning and preparing your Christmas display way in advance - which does not mean the first week of December, but months and months earlier. You want to be thinking about how everything's going to come together when everyone else is wondering how many hamburgers, hot dogs, and cans of beer they can consume at their 4th of July picnic and still be awake (or alive) for the fireworks that night.

Just like most industries that are devoted to one specific time of year, Christmas light and decor suppliers host big sales throughout the year that are dedicated to decorators who plan way ahead of time and who want to grab everything they need early so they can get what they want at the best price and before inventory starts to run low – which happens VERY quickly in October and November.

If you do your homework, you will find that stores like The Christmas Light Emporium have periodic big sales throughout the year. The megastores will give everyone a big break on Black Friday, but that's usually already cutting it a bit close. There are also sales throughout the summer as these big franchises look to reduce inventory to make room for the new stuff. That's a perfect time to stock up at a discounted rate and remove a lot of worry from your budget.

Make sure you've got somewhere to store all your stuff, so don't forget about it by the time decorating season rolls around. My wife is famous for buying Christmas presents months in advance and then forgetting where she hid them. One year, we gave out two presents in mid-March as a make-believe "good behavior" award, but it was really because we found them while cleaning out a closet.

It's not just sales you should be on the lookout for, but also any loyalty programs or exclusive offers that Christmas light suppliers may have. Most of them are as simple to unlock as adding your email and/or phone number, and then you're in business as one of the fancy folks who knows 72 hours in advance when everything is about to go on sale. These little perks can go a long way towards softening the blow on your budget.

Drawing and Measuring

I talked a few paragraphs back about being an artist. The good news is that you don't have to be Picasso to draw a rudimentary picture of your yard and house and sketch out how you want to lay out your display. You need to be handy with a tape measure - the traditional kind or the fancy laser pointer - and be able to draw relatively to scale to ensure everything will fit in the space you want it to fit in. Before you start any master plan, you need to get a feel for your property regarding measurements. There's no dumber feeling in the world than realizing that you're about 50 lights too short of the effect you're trying to create or that you want to hang the giant wreath 15 feet up on your house, but the ladder only gets you to 10 feet.

Measure EVERYTHING, then measure it again! When it comes time to hang the lights, you'll be efficient and confident in what you're doing. Plus, when you're installing lights in broad daylight, every work-from-home neighbor has their eyes on you, and every Ring security system is casually recording your every move. Unless you want to wind up on the next installment of Fail Army as *"guy who almost chokes himself while installing Christmas lights"*, it's a very, very good idea to plan ahead.

How to Measure Roof Outlines, Trees, Bushes, and More

Roof Fascia and Peaks

I get it—climbing ladders or spending hours up on your roof, measuring every nook and cranny, sounds about as appealing as eating that fruitcake Aunt Sue gifted last Christmas, right? Maybe a bit terrifying, too. But hey, here's some good news! Our pals at Google have come to the rescue with a nifty tool that lets you estimate your roof measurements faster than you can say "fruitcake." And the best part? No ladders, no roofs, heck, you don't even have to step outside!

1. First things first, plop yourself down in that ultra-comfy chair in front of your trusty computer. Make it feel like you're settling in for a Netflix binge.

2. Fire up your web browser and mosey on over to google.com. Type your address into the search bar and give that 'enter' key a satisfying tap.

3. Voilà, you should see a page filled with goodies related to your address. Right at the top, there's a map with a cute little red pin marking your territory. Click on that map like you're clicking on the last cookie in the jar.

4. Now, you should be gazing at a glorious, larger satellite view of the map with that red pin showing your humble abode. Feel like a satellite spy yet?

5. Zoom in like you're trying to read the fine print on a shady contract. Use the "+" symbol in the lower right corner or the magical powers of your mouse.

6. Pick the spot on your roof where you want to start your measuring adventure. Choose wisely—it's like picking your favorite ice cream flavor.

7. Here comes the fun part: right-click on your starting point with the mouse. A menu pops up, and guess what? One of those options is "measure distance." Select it, and ta-da! A little white dot appears like a breadcrumb on your map.

8. Now, left-click your way around the outline of your house. Watch as the total length appears at the bottom center of your screen like a magician pulling a rabbit out of a hat.

You can now measure anything you want that is visible on your property via Google Satellite View! You can find a quick video walk-through I made for you here: https://iam.christmas/using-google-satellite-view-to-measure-your-roof/

Once you have all your measurements, add them up to get the total length of light stringers you will need for your roof lights.

Walking Path, Driveway, and Flower Bed Outlines

Add a sprinkle of festive magic to your home by lining walkways, flower beds, driveways, and sidewalks with C7 or C9 Christmas lights! Here's a simple step-by-step guide to ensure you have just the right amount of lights to make your house the star of the neighborhood:

1. Gather Your Tools: Arm yourself with a measuring tape, notepad, pen, and a trusty sidekick to lend a hand. Trust me, this could be a bonding moment—or at least a chance to argue over who gets to hold the tape.

2. Flower Beds: Begin your quest by measuring the perimeter of each flower bed. Channel your inner gardener and note down the distance. Rinse and repeat for all flower beds you aim to dazzle.

3. Pathway Planning: For paths, drag your tape along the edge you want to light up, navigating any twists and turns like a pro. Keep track of each path's total length as you go.

4. Driveways: Measure both sides from start to finish with precision. Driveways come in all shapes and sizes, so don't forget those wacky curves.

5. Sidewalk Stretch: Stretch your tape along your sidewalks' sides, and don't get tangled in corners or turns. A seamless light show awaits if you capture this measurement spot-on.

6. Do the Math: Sum up your measurements. Each C7 or C9 light string covers a specific lit length (hint: check the box or packaging they came in). Divide your total length by one string's lit length to find out how

many you'll need. Easy-peasy!

7. Plan for Extras: Seriously, get an extra string or two. Better to have a couple of stragglers than to be left in the dark when you're one string short.

>>>>> **PRO TIP** <<<<<

Remember that C7 and C9 light strings come in various lengths of space between the sockets. The most common are 6 inches and 12 inches, but some have 15 inches, 18 inches, or even 24 inches between each socket. The most common spacing for walkways, driveways, and outlines is 12 inches.

Bushes/Shrubs

String Lights vs. Net Lights

Alright, folks, decision time. You gotta pick your fighter: string lights or net lights for those bushes and shrubs. If you're a control freak who loves precision, string lights are your jam. They're your best bet for those odd-shaped bushes, ensuring your display looks like it belongs in a holiday magazine.

If you're more of a "get it done quick" person, grab some net lights. They come in standard sizes (usually 4 feet x 6 feet) with a bulb spacing of 4 or 6 inches, letting you drape them over larger bushes in a flash. The catch? They rarely fit perfectly, so if you're a perfectionist, skip the nets and stick to the strings.

Now for the Measuring

1. **Gather Your Tools**: Start with a flexible tape measure, a notepad, and a pen. Additionally, have a calculator on hand (there is one built into

almost all smartphones) for quick calculations.

2. **Measure the Dimensions**:

    a. **Height**: Measure from the base of the bush or shrub to the top.

    b. **Width and Depth**: Find the widest and deepest part of the bush, typically near the center. This gives you the full circumference you'll be working with.

3. **Calculate the Number of Lights Strings or Net Lights You Will Need**

Before you can determine how many sets of string lights or net lights you will need, you need to know the spacing between the bulbs and the total lit length of the string, or, if you're using net lights, the spacing, lit width, and depth of your net light set. You can usually find this information on the fancy packaging that the lights come in, on the website of the store you bought them from, or on the manufacturer's website.

String Light Example

Let's talk string lights. Imagine you've got a 23-foot-long light string with bulbs spaced 4 inches apart. You want to maintain that 4-inch spacing on your bushes. So, for a bush that's 48 inches wide, 36 inches tall, and 24 inches deep, here's the game plan:

Assume you're wrapping horizontally from the back left to the front and over to the back right, and horizontally across the top:

- **Top**: ((48 inches wide x 24 inches deep) / 4-inch spacing) = 288 inches of lights

- **Sides**: ((36 inches high x 24 inches deep) / 4-inch spacing) x 2 sides = 432 inches of lights

- **Front**: ((48 inches wide x 36 inches high) / 4-inch spacing) = 432 inches of lights

Add it all up: 288 + 432 + 432 = 1152 inches of lights. Divide by 12 to get 96 feet of lights needed. With 23-foot strings, you'll need about 4.17 strings.

>>>>>   **PRO TIP**   <<<<<

When measuring your roof, bushes, driveway or anything else to determine how much light or garland or other material you will need, always round up or add 10-20% to avoid any "Oops, I'm short" moments.

Net Light Example

Net lights are like the fast food of holiday decorating—quick, convenient, and you might need a nap after. They usually come in a 4 feet x 6 feet size. Using the same bush dimensions, if you skip covering the sides, you're just working with the 24-inch top depth, 36-inch height, and 48-inch width. That's 5 feet tall x 4 feet wide.

With standard net lights, one set draped longways covers the front and top, leaving a foot of excess hanging down the back. Talk about easy-breezy!

Door and Window Outlines

Get ready to deck the halls with flair! Transform your home into a festive wonderland by following this easy-peasy guide to measuring your doors and windows. You'll be the envy of the block with your pro-level decorations!

Measuring a Door Outline

1. **Gather Your Tools**: Grab a measuring tape, a notepad, and a pencil. Voilà, your holiday toolkit!

2. **Start at the Top**: Measure across the top of the door frame from one edge to the other. Write it down, no cheating!

3. **Measure the Side Edges**: Measure one side from the top to your desired endpoint. Repeat on the other side. Record these numbers like they're the digits to Santa's workshop!

4. **Calculate Total Length**: Add your top and side measurements together. That's how much bling you'll need!

Example: Got an 8-foot-tall door that's 4 feet wide? You'll need 20 feet of lights or greenery. Easy-peasy! Most pro-grade garlands are 9 feet long, perfect for outlining your door and having a foot or so of space at the bottom on each side of your door.

>>>>> **PRO TIP** <<<<<

When hanging garland around a door or window, you can add a more professional touch by slightly swagging the top. By adding a nail or screw on the left corner and another at the right corner that is parallel and then adding a third screw at the center above your door about 2-4 inches higher than the corners, you can allow the garland or lights to slightly swag, creating a really professional look. Some folks even like to add mistletoe or a bow at the high center point of the swag for even more pizzazz!

Measuring a Window Outline

1. **Gather Your Supplies**: Just like with the door, tape measure, notepad, pencil. You got this!

2. **Measure the Top Edge**: Run that tape from corner to corner on the top. Note it!

3. **Measure Both Sides**: Each side deserves attention too. Top to bottom, folks.

4. **Don't Forget the Bottom Edge**: You betcha, windows get the full treatment. Measure across the bottom and jot that down.

5. **Combine Measurements**: Total up the top, sides, and bottom to know how long your light string or garland needs to be.

Example: A 4x5-foot window needs 18 feet of lighting. When measuring your window outlines, consider each window separately since you will want to install a separate run of lights for each window.

>>>>>   **PRO TIP**   <<<<<

Pro installers will almost always use 6-inch spaced C7 bulbs and strings to outline doors and windows while using 12-inch spaced C9 bulbs to outline roof fascia and peaks.

Trees: Trunk Wraps, Canopy Wraps, and Branch Wraps

When it comes to determining how many lights you need to wrap a tree, it all depends on *HOW* you intend to wrap the tree! So, let's first explore the most common ways professional installers wrap outdoor trees with Christmas lights.

Trunk Wraps

We'll start with the trunk wrap, the easiest method to measure and install. So, what is a trunk wrap? A trunk wrap is a festive and eye-catching technique to enhance a tree's natural beauty by spiraling strands of lights tightly around the tree's trunk and only its trunk, stopping the lights just under the canopy or slightly up into the canopy.

This method starts at the base and involves wrapping lights evenly upwards, ensuring a consistent glow. It creates a dramatic focal point in any outdoor display and sets the stage for expanding your holiday decor onto branches and canopies. Trunk wraps emphasize the silhouette of a tree, transforming it into a mesmerizing beacon of holiday cheer that captivates anyone who passes by. It is also the quickest and easiest method to install because, in most cases, you don't need to reach very high up the tree or even need a ladder.

To figure out how many light strings you need to trunk wrap a tree, you will first need to know the following:

1. The lit length of the light strings you intend to use - in inches

2. The bulb spacing on the light strings you intend to use - in inches

3. The height of the tree trunk you are wrapping - in inches

4. The width (diameter) of the tree trunk you are wrapping - in inches. Most trees don't have a consistent diameter, so making an educated guess or using an average across multiple measurement points is acceptable.

Example: You have a 6-foot (72-inch) tall tree trunk with an 8-inch diameter that you want to wrap with 70 bulb strings at 4-inch spacing. The lit length of your lights is 23 feet.

First, you will need to calculate the circumference of your tree trunk. Circumference is calculated as diameter x pi. So, in this example, the circumference of your tree trunk is 8 x 3.14 = 25.12 inches.

The height divided by your desired spacing will equal the number of times around the trunk you need to wrap the lights

- 72 inches (height)/4 inches (spacing)=18 times around the trunk

- 18 times around the trunk when the trunk is 25.12 in circumference: 18 x 25.12 = 452.16 inches of lights required to wrap your trunk with 4-inch spacing

- Convert your total inches (452.16) to feet: 452.16/12 = 37.68 feet

- Your light strings have a lit length of 23 feet, so to get your required number of light strings, divide the total feet by the length of your light string: 37.68/23 = 1.63 strings of lights

- As always, round your final number up. So, in this example, you will need 2 strings of 70 lights with 4-inch spacing.

>>>>> **PRO TIP** <<<<<

The most common type, length, and spacing of light strings that professional installers use for wrapping trees are 5mm LED strings with 70 bulbs and 4-inch spacing, or 5mm LED strings with 50 bulbs and 6-inch spacing. The most elegant displays will always use 70-bulb strings with 4-inch spacing. However, 50-bulb strings with 6-inch spacing will cost less. So, if you are budget-conscious, this maybe a good option for you.

Canopy Wraps

If you want to wrap your tree all the way to the top, the quickest, easiest, and most affordable way is to wrap or drape lights around the exterior of the tree's canopy.

What is a tree canopy? A tree canopy is the uppermost layer of foliage that forms the total span of branches and leaves of a tree, creating a natural "roof" above the trunk.

Canopy wraps are a popular choice for many because they provide a stunning overhead display of lights that creates a magical, enchanting atmosphere with minimal effort. Some folks prefer to wrap canopies instead of meticulously wrapping each branch for a few compelling reasons. Firstly, canopy wraps are faster and require less precise work, making them an efficient option for decorating larger trees or multiple trees. Rather than wrapping each branch individually, which can be time-consuming and labor-intensive, the canopy method delivers a beautiful, cohesive appearance with fewer light strings and considerably less effort.

Instead of painstakingly dressing each branch, you simply drape and wrap lights around the exterior of the canopy, achieving a dazzling, cohesive look with fewer strands and less effort than a full branch wrap. So, grab your lights, skip the tree yoga, and let your tree shine like a star!

Estimating the number of light strings to wrap around your tree canopy is like trying to guess how many jellybeans are in a jar—it's a bit of a gamble! The pros might have a sixth sense for it, but for the rest of us, here's a top-secret formula to get you started:

1. Estimate the total height of your canopy from the bottom of the canopy to the top (in feet).

2. Estimate the width of your canopy at the bottom, the middle, and about 75% of the way to the top (in feet).

3. Decide how much spacing you want to have between the strings in the canopy (in feet).

4. Calculate the average circumference (in feet) - remember that circumference is diameter x pi (3.14).

5. Divide the height of your canopy (in feet) by your desired spacing between strings (in feet) to determine the number of times you need to wrap around your canopy.

6. Multiply the average circumference (in feet) times the number of times

you need to wrap around your canopy to determine the total length of lighting you will need.

Example time! Picture this: your tree stands proud at 12 feet tall, with widths of 8 feet at the bottom, 5 feet in the middle, and 2 feet near the top. You're opting for a cozy 1-foot spacing between strings. Here's the math magic:

- Average circumference: (8 + 5 + 2) / 3 = 5 feet average diameter. 5 x 3.14(pi) = 15.7 average circumference.

- Number of times around the canopy: 12 (canopy height) / 1 (spacing) = 12 times around the canopy.

- Total lighting: 15.7 (average circumference) x 12 (loops) = 188.4 feet of festive glow.

Using string lights with 70 bulbs at a snazzy 4-inch spacing, like our trunk wrap example, divide your needed length by your string's lit length (23 feet in this instance) to get the number of strings: 188.4 / 23 = 8.19. I'd round up to 10 because it's better to have extra sparkle than not enough!

If you are using a 2-wire socket stringer (C7 or C9 light strings with removable screw-in bulbs), just make sure you have a total length of socket stringer as needed. In this example, I would round up to 200 feet.

Branch Wraps

Branch wraps are the ultimate showstopper for your tree canopy—challenging, time-consuming, pricey, but oh-so-gorgeous! If you're armed with the time, budget, tools, and a sprinkle of determination, go for it. Trust me, you'll get more compliments on a perfectly branch-wrapped tree than on your grandma's secret pie recipe. Picture this: a tree so beautifully wrapped it looks like it was sprinkled with Christmas magic, each branch shimmering with delight. Stunning is an understatement.

But hold onto your Santa hat because this isn't a walk in the park. Branch wrapping is the marathon of holiday decorating—patience and precision are your best friends here. And yep, it can cost a pretty penny given the zillion lights and expensive gear you'll need, especially for really big trees. Prepare for a time warp where hours turn into days. Yet, despite this Herculean effort, the jaw-dropping final result is worth every bit of the sweat and sparkle!

> >>>>> **PRO TIP** <<<<<
>
> *If you decide to go all out and branch-wrap your outdoor tree but need to keep the budget and time requirement in check, skip some of the mid-size and smaller branches that form the canopy of a tree. By focusing only on the major branches in your tree canopy (usually the widest and longest branches), you can shave 50% off the time and cost of a fully branch-wrapped tree. And no one will notice the unwrapped smaller branches.*

Determining what length of lights you need to completely and fully branch-wrap your tree is not easy. No equation or firm mathematics can reasonably be used to make an estimate. Pro installers struggle with this and make a point of heavily overestimating the length of lighting that will be required to ensure they are not caught short on lights.

But there is a way to put a little method behind the madness. Think of your tree canopy as nothing more than a series of connected tree TRUNKS. Here's the math:

1. Make a list of each major tree branch you want to wrap

2. Calculate the number of lights you would need to wrap each branch if it were a stand-alone trunk wrap (see the section above on how to calculate light lengths for trunk wraps)

3. Once you have the length of lights needed for each of your major branches, add them together

4. Then add 30% to your total length for all branches you want to wrap

5. Divide the total length you need by the lit length of the strings you intend to use to wrap your branches to get an estimate of the total

number of strings you will need

Example: The hard part is making a list of your large branches and their dimensions and calculating the required string lengths for each branch (*see the section on trunk wraps above*). But once you have this magic number. It's simple math.

Picture this: you've got a tree that could double as a mini forest, with 17 branches all shouting, "Wrap me!" You've made a list, measured each branch as a trunk wrap, and tallied the total length of lights you need. You came up with a total length across all 17 branches - drum roll, please—it's a whopping 14,076 inches! The light string you want to use (I recommend a 5mm LED string with 70 bulbs and 4-inch spacing between bulbs) has a lit length of 23 feet.

1. First up, convert those inches to feet because, well, math: 14076 / 12 = 1173 feet.

2. Next, divide and conquer: total feet needed by the lit length of your string: 1173 / 23 = 51 sets of lights.

Voilà! You're now the proud owner of the most *lit* tree on the block!

Pine Trees: A Special Type of Tree

Pine trees are usually treated differently than other types of trees when lighting them up for Christmas. This is because a pine tree canopy comes all the way to the ground (in many cases, anyway). Some don't. But even those that don't are still unique in that their canopy is far more uniform in shape than any other type of tree. It's a cone - the quintessential Christmas tree.

If your pine tree has a trunk, you can measure the length of lights needed for it using the trunk-wrap method we discussed a couple of sections back. For this section, I'll focus on the canopy of your pine tree.

There are two other BIG differences between pine trees and most other trees:

1. The branches usually don't lose their 'leaves' in the winter.

2. They have relatively weak branches that don't have the strength to support a branch wrap method.

This is why you never see a pine tree with every branch wrapped in Christmas lights. It's pretty much impossible, thanks to physics. So, almost all outdoor pine trees are strung with lights in pretty much exactly the same way you would wrap lights around your indoor Christmas tree. Just a lot more lights.

The math required to figure out how many lights you will need for wrapping around your giant outdoor pine tree is exactly the same as for your 8-foot-tall indoor Christmas tree and is very similar to the calculation for determining lengths for trunk wraps.

You need to know:

1. The lit length of the lit strings you intend to use - in inches.

2. The bulb spacing on the light strings you intend to use - in inches.

3. The height of the tree trunk you are wrapping - in inches.

4. The average width (diameter) of the pine canopy you are wrapping - in inches. With pine trees, you will need to ballpark the width of the canopy at 50% of the way up the tree from the bottom of the canopy. This will be your average diameter.

Example: You have a 15-foot (180-inch) pine tree canopy with an 8-foot (96-inch) wide average diameter (diameter at the center of the canopy) that you want to wrap with C9 bulbs that are spaced 12 inches apart. You also want to use C9 stringers with a lit length of 99 feet (100 bulbs).

First, you will need to calculate the average circumference of your pine tree canopy.

Circumference is calculated as diameter x pi. So, in this example, the average circumference of your pine tree canopy is 96 x 3.14 = 301.44 inches.

The height divided by your desired spacing will equal the number of times around the canopy you need to wrap the lights.

1. 180 inches (height)/12 inches (spacing) = 15 times around the canopy.

2. 15 times around the canopy when the canopy is 304.44 in average circumference: 15 x 304.44 = 4,566 inches of lights required to wrap your canopy with 12-inch spacing.

3. Convert your total inches (4,566) to feet: 4566/12 = 380.5 feet.

4. Your light stringers have a lit length of 99 feet, so to get your required number of light strings, divide the total feet by the length of your light string: 380.5/99 = 3.84 strings of lights.

5. As always, round your final number up. In this example, you will need 4 strings of 100 C9 bulbs with 12-inch spacing.

>>>>> **PRO TIP** <<<<<

To determine how many light strings you need for a pine tree (indoor or outdoor), hop on over to The Christmas Light Emporium website and use Rudolph's Christmas Tree Light String Calculator! It will provide you with the number of strings you need for your pine tree, with no math required! It will calculate the number of strings you need for each type of light string and any pine tree with a canopy base up to 15 feet wide and a canopy height up to 30 feet.

And there you have it—everything you need to create a holiday display that'll have your neighbors looking on in envy and awe. Measure like a pro, decorate like a legend!

Make Your List, Check it Twice

You must have a list before you start shopping. Anything else is just absolutely the worst idea. How do I know? Because I've been that guy who goes to the grocery store without a list - and while absolutely starving. When I did that, I decided that after all these years, I'd secretly been missing the asparagus and Brussels sprouts I was forced to eat as a child, and I bought five cans of each – yes, canned Brussels spouts! Fast-forward 6 months, and those cans were still in the pantry, and I was left wondering why I was such an idiot.

During the holiday decorating season, Christmas light and decoration stores are to adults what toy stores and toy catalogs are to kids: irresistible. These retailers know that if you're in the store or on the site, you've already got a pretty strong interest in making a purchase. So they're going to place all of their finest 'geegaws and gadgets,' as my grandmother liked to say, out on the shelves to attract your attention and loosen your purse strings. If you don't have a hard and fast list in front of you, you're going to make a lot of purchases ostensibly, and the idea that you can continue to keep straight what you actually need becomes laughable. You'll go home with 17 reindeer, a menorah that plays "Who Let the Dogs Out," and a rapping Mary and Joseph combination that break dances all over the Nativity.

Your list should contain many things. One is a checklist for the tools and other periphery equipment you'll need, one is a checklist for the actual display items you'll need, and the third is a bank page to make notes on for the million times that things don't work out as you planned. It might sound rudimentary, but things will get complicated. The list tells you exactly where you're at, what's needed, and what you have enough of. So, remember to make these lists:

- Tools and basic supplies

- Lights, decor and display items and accessories

- Blank page for notes and adjustments

Once you've got it all organized, get out there and start looking for the best deals on the things you need. Stick to your list religiously. You're going to see a lot of things that seem like they'd be wonderful to add, but don't fall victim. As esteemed Rebel Alliance military leader Admiral Ackbar once said, "It's a trap!"

Don't be an impulse buyer at this stage. If you see things that look cool or would be a great accessory to your plan, copy/paste the link, bookmark them, or dog ear that page in the catalog, but don't buy them yet. They are not part of your budget, which means at this point in time, they do not even exist. Your goal is to get all the things you need at or below the budget that you've laid out for yourself. Nothing more. Nothing less.

If you've acquired everything you need (your lists!) and still have some money left in your budget, you can do one of two things.

1. Put it into an emergency fund that you will very likely dip into the first time something breaks or fizzles out or doesn't stretch or doesn't wrap or a million other problems that are going to have you wishing you had a rapid-transit system built under your driveway that took you directly to Home Depot or Lowe's.

2. Buy *ONE* thing of the many items that you wanted to buy while you were shopping for your supplies. Buy only that one thing that you think will best accentuate the excellent plan that you already have in place and that you have been working hard on these many weeks and months. Don't throw all that time and

labor away for the 19-foot tall inflatable Vecna from "Stranger Things" wearing a Santa hat and singing "Holly, Jolly Christmas" just because you think it will freak out your kids. You're falling victim to the same thing I've talked about repeatedly — the dreaded impulse purchase. You have a written-out budget for a reason, and it's not to waste it on things that you're easily distracted brain suddenly thinks would make you King or Queen of the Neighborhood. Stick to the plan, and everything will work out for the best. There's always next year for Vecna.

Chapter Ten

Installation Tips & Techniques

This is the Big **M** Moment, folks. *Capital M*, because this isn't just any moment—this is the one where you weave together all those threads of effort and finally enjoy the fruits of your labor. But hold on before you start strutting your stuff in front of the neighbors and claiming the title of World's Greatest Decorator. First, you must stick to a solid plan that ensures everything is ready to roll. This way, when you get to the actual task, it's a breeze, takes less time, and you won't be caught off guard without a crucial piece. It's all about being prepared, like a master chef who doesn't want to realize halfway through cooking that the eggs are still at the store.

If you're anything like me, you've probably had that moment in adulthood when your significant other drops the bomb: they've bought some new piece of furniture online, and guess what? You're now the designated assembly expert because it's like 957% cheaper that way. Fast forward a few hours—you're drenched in sweat in your living room, swearing like a sailor (enough to send one of the kids into tears), and adding yet another Allen wrench to the collection in your utility drawer. Voilà, the masterpiece is finally done. Cue the realization: there are about

6 or 7 washers, nuts, or screws that didn't make the cut. Then, just when you think you're in the clear, your spouse notes that one piece is on backward, making the whole thing look like garbage. That's usually my cue to deflect and suggest that maybe a professional builder would have nailed it, but alas, you're stuck with me. We trade a few unpleasantries for about two minutes, followed by a 2–8-hour cone of silence. Maybe I've said too much.

You've poured way too much blood, sweat, and glitter into your Christmas display to start slapping things together all willy-nilly now. Seriously, remember that time you tangled with the lights and lost? Exactly. So, let's get our hard hats on and make this holiday magic happen like a boss!

Laying the Groundwork

- Lay out everything you will use in a safe, secure space.

- Place all your tools in one spot

- Place all your extension cords in another spot

- Screw your bulbs into your C7 and/or C9 stringers. Some types of clips require that you install them onto the string at the same time you screw the bulb into the socket. So make sure you do this if you are using this style of clip, like the Tuff Clip brand of light clips. It may seem like a hassle, but they are the best clips around, will not fall off, make takedown a breeze, and contain a UV inhibitor that guarantees they will last for many years.

- Place all your light strings in a third

- Unpack your light strings and roll them into balls (*see the PRO TIP below!*)

- Place your balled-up light strings into labeled storage tubs, so you're never wasting time searching for one or the other

- Make sure your extension cords are all the same relative color. It will look weird and unprofessional if there are seven orange ones, 12 green ones, three black ones, and a white one right in the middle.

>>>>> **PRO TIP** <<<<<

Roll all of your light strings into balls. Be sure to start with the female plug end so the male end is on the outside of your balled string. Roll them into a ball, not a doughnut. Doughnuts are bad for you. Doughnut. Bad. This will make installation of your lights much easier. Roll them back up the same way when you take them down. It makes storage and maintenance much easier.

Install Your Lights and Décor

Keep these things in mind:

- The techniques, notes, and commentary I include here are just the tip of the iceberg. They are intended as a starting point. These tips and techniques will be more than you need for most display designs. But if you have designed a Christmas display that can be seen from Mars, you will likely encounter questions or problems that are not addressed here. In that case, I recommend reaching out to your local decorating group for advice from other experienced decorators near you.

- Get to work early in the day, especially when the weather is nice - meaning there is little chance of rain, wind, and no winter wonderland climates like snow, ice, sleet, or hail.

- If you're using a ladder, get someone to spot you – ideally, someone strong enough and old enough to hold a ladder still.

- Do one task at a time instead of randomly mixing or matching. That's a great way to get sloppy as you switch from one mindset to another. It also lets you feel like you are accomplishing pieces of a puzzle, like that debt strategy where you pay off your smallest credit card debt first and then move on to the next one. Making steady progress and being able to check off items from your list is a positive reminder that you are building something great and getting closer to the finish line.

The following installation tips and techniques will probably be more complex than your to-do list. Still, I wanted to make it reasonably comprehensive with some notes regarding best practices for each type of item installation. Feel free to skip the areas I cover that don't apply to your design. Better yet, add them to your list for next year! Remember, there's no such thing as too many Christmas lights!

>>>>> **PRO TIP** <<<<<

Before we start with your installation, I need to tell you the single most important thing you need to know about making your own extension cords and using SPT wire with slide on plugs. **NEVER INSTALL A MALE PLUG ON BOTH ENDS OF A PIECE OF WIRE OR SOCKET STRINGER!!!!!** *We call this a* **'suicide string'**. *If you do this and you, or one of your helpers, decide to plug one end into a hot electrical source, you will then have two hot metal prongs on the other end. This could lead to serious consequences, including electrical shock, severe injuries, or fire. Don't do this ever, for any reason.*

Gather your Supplies

By now, you should have made your lists, checked them twice, completed your shopping, and organized everything. You are ready to tackle your installation!

For most folks, a basic installation of roof lights and some yard decor can be accomplished in one day. But for some, with displays that can be seen from space, it will take many days, sometimes even weeks, to install your extravaganza. Be mindful of which parts of your display you will install on which days. Make a schedule of which tools and decor you will need to have ready for each day's work. This way, you aren't dragging out everything in the garage just to hang some net lights on your bushes!

With that in mind, here is a list of the supplies and tools you will likely need to have at-the-ready no matter what type of decor you install on any given day.

- **Light stringers** with the bulbs already screwed into their sockets. Depending on the clip style you decide to use, the clips might also be already installed onto the string (see 'Laying the Groundwork' above).

- **Light Strings** for wrapping tree trunks, installing into wreaths or garlands, wrapping around columns, and lots of other potential uses depending on your display design.

- **Light Clips.** If you are using the more common omniclip or all-application clip, or any variety of gutter clip, shingle tab, magnetic clip, or mini clip, you'll need those for installing your lights along your roof line, gutters, or fascia. If you intend also to install lights on your ridges, you will need to have some ridge clips handy as well. Lawn stakes for pathway and driveway outlines, C-clips for installing lighting along wood fences, etc. Make sure you have the clips you will need for each day's project.

- **Bulk Wire.** You'll need some bulk SPT wire handy for making jumpers (see Chapter 2) and for making extension cords that run from your power sources up to each part of your display that requires power.

- **Slide On Vampire Plugs.** You'll need male and female plugs for sure.

And, if you need to make any jumpers, inline female plugs will help make it much easier, safer, and sturdier when you install them into the middle of a wire run without cutting the wire. The result will be a female plug in the middle of your wire. You can then plug another run of lights into it and run them in a different direction or a jumper to another part of your roof without interrupting the straight line of the original string it feeds from. Female inline plugs are also a key tool for use in powering your display (see more later in this chapter about powering your display).

- **Tool Belt:** I use a tool belt to carry slide-on plugs around while installing lights. This way, they are always within easy reach and separated by plug type. Look for a tool belt with four pockets: one for male plugs, one for female plugs, one for inline female plugs, and the fourth for the slide-on caps.

- **Zip Ties:** Keep a stash of a few zip ties in your tool belt. They come in handy for all sorts of things, including temporarily securing loose wires. When running your power source up to your roof, you can run the wire up a gutter downspout and secure it by wrapping a zip tie around it in 2-4 spots. They can be used for hanging wreaths, garland, cleaning up extension cord spaghetti and all sorts of things. Keep them handy at all times.

- **Cutters/Dikes:** Keep a good pair of cutters in your tool belt at all times. They make cutting your wire to length and snipping the ends off of zip ties a breeze.

- **Ladder or Roof Boots:** If you plan to install your lights around your roof line from the ground and use a ladder, be sure to have a second person available to spot you and hold the ladder steady. If you work from on top of the roof, you will benefit from a good pair of roofer's boots.

I recommend the Cougar Paws brand. You might also need a ladder for other areas of your installation, including windows, doors or tall trees.

Rooflines and Ridges

Nothing like getting up there early in the morning and knocking this one out first. I like to do it when I'm fresh mentally so I don't risk a misstep or a bad idea that results in starting over or hanging upside down twisting in the wind.

The size of your roof will determine 1) How many bulbs you will need and 2) how many power sources you will need. I don't recommend running more than 100 bulbs from a single power source. Some folks disagree with me and will swear they efficiently run up to 300 LED bulbs from a single power run. This all depends on how much power must be pulled through the entire length of the wire to power all the lights. If you're feeling risky, make sure that your wire has a load rating that is high enough and you have calculated what your power drop will be over distance. Otherwise, I always recommend sticking to the rule of 100: at most, 100 bulbs per run. Follow this rule, and you'll be fine.

If you follow the rule of 100 and you have 225 lights at 12-inch spacing (225 feet of lights), then I would recommend two separate power runs: one for the first 100 feet and another for the remaining 125 feet.

Install Your Roof Lights!

1. Begin at an outlet to ensure you have a power source nearby. Attach the clips to the light string (if they aren't already) and start placing them along the roofline, ensuring they're evenly spaced. Secure each clip before moving to the next to prevent sagging.

2. Install any needed jumpers as you go along.

3. If you are installing lights on the ridges of your roof, install those after your roof line has been installed. Either run a separate extension cord to the beginning of your ridge run or (if your run of lights is less than or around 100 bulbs!) tie the start of your ridge run into an existing roof line string or jumper using an inline female plug on the source string and a male plug at the start of your ridge run.

Window and Doorway Outlines

Outlining your windows and doorways with lights or greenery is a great way to add depth to your Christmas displays. It creates a nice transition from lawn decor to roof lighting. But installing them can often be a bit tricky. Here are some guidelines for dealing with the most common types of surfaces for window and doorway outlines.

>>>>> **PRO TIP** <<<<<

To power a lit wreath hanging in the middle of a door, make sure the wire is long enough to let the door swing all the way open – preferably, use dark wire for a dark door or white or light color for a light color door. This way, the door will retain its full ability to swing open while remaining as 'invisible' as possible. I recommend running a separate extension cord for your wreaths. Run the extension cord up one side of your doorway and swag the power down from the top corner of the hinged side of the door.

>>> **BONUS TIP** <<<

Installing a garland around your door will provide a nice place to hide the extension cord that powers your door wreath.

If you are lighting up multiple windows and doors, some of which are relatively close together, create jumpers from one to the next and drop a single male plug to the ground - this allows you to power more than one window/door from a single power run when they are close together. You will come back later to tie all of these male plugs into a single run to your power source.

Remember that attaching lights around doors and windows almost always leaves minor damage to the surface. Be it screwing light clips into the wood framing or hot gluing sockets to brick surfaces. These techniques will likely leave some damage behind when you take them down, even if it's just a tiny hole from a screw that holds a clip in place or a spot on your brick that gets pulled off when you remove the hot glue. If you want to keep your window and door frames 100% damage-free, I recommend skipping the lights, as there aren't many ways to guarantee a damage-free installation of lights around most windows and doors.

Wood Surfaces

Attaching light sockets to wooden surfaces can be a breeze with the right approach. Use light clips tailored for wooden surfaces for a secure fit - like a C-Clip. These clips can either be nailed gently or screwed in, providing a stable base for your light strings. And the screw holes are relatively easy to repair if you ever need to. Some folks choose to use staples to hold light stringers in place around wood windows and door frames. The holes will be smaller, but there will be a lot more of them. So keep that in mind when deciding on which technique to use.

Vinyl Siding

Vinyl surfaces pose a different challenge. Opt for vinyl siding hooks, which allow you to secure the lights without causing any damage. These hooks slide easily between the siding slats and hold the lights snugly in place, making removal post-holidays a non-hassle ordeal!

Brick Surfaces

Brick requires some creativity. Adhesive clips work wonders on smooth brick surfaces. However, if the brick is textured, use masonry clips that grip the edge of the bricks. These methods avoid the need for drilling, gluing or using nails, maintaining the integrity of your brick.

>>>>> **PRO TIP** <<<<<

Pros and Cons of Hot Glue or Staples

Hot glue offers a quick and strong adhesion for affixing lights to surfaces such as wood or brick. For this reason, it is a popular technique. But the downside of using hot glue is that it will almost always leave some damage behind when you take the lights down.

Staples are also popular for securing light strings to wood surfaces. It is fast and offers a secure installation option. But, like hot glue (or even screwing in a C-Clip), it will leave some damage behind in the form of small holes that will have to be repaired at some point.

By choosing the appropriate method for each surface type and understanding the nuances of each technique, you can achieve a vibrant and dazzling holiday display! Your windows and doorways will shine brightly, reflecting your holiday spirit for all to see!

Architectural Features (columns, etc.)

There are many fun ways to light up other architectural features of your property. One of my favorites is to use flood lights or spotlights placed on the ground, pointing up at the feature you want to highlight. It's fast, easy, and leaves no damage.

When wrapping lights or garland around columns, I always recommend using zip ties to secure the lights or garland at the bottom, the top, and one or two spots up the column. You can connect multiple zip ties together until you get a length that works for your application. Pull them snug, and they will hold your lights, garlands, and other decor in place all season long. Don't forget to use your trusty cutters/dikes to trim off the ends of your zip ties for a clean look.

And remember to always start with your male plug at the bottom. Unless you have a unique reason for placing your male plug at the top of a column, your life will be much easier when all your male plugs are at ground level. One example of an exception might be if you have a second-story balcony and you want to power the first-floor columns under the balcony from a power source that is ON the second-floor balcony. In a case like this, it might be easier to install your column lighting with the male plug at the top of the column.

Pathway and Flow Bed Outlines

Pathway lighting: the underrated hero of outdoor glow-ups! Forget about roof lights that turn you into Spider-Man scaling your house—pathway lighting keeps your feet firmly on the ground. Seriously, just grab some C7 or C9 bulbs and those top-tier stringers. It's so straightforward that even your dog might try to join in the fun! No need for ladders, just take a leisurely stroll down the path of brilliance!

The only unique tool you'll need is a series of handy lawn stakes. Most lawn stakes will fit either C7 or C9 sockets. You'll need one stake for each bulb along your path. A handy and sturdy 5-inch lawn stake will be perfect if you live in a snow-free climate. But if you live in a place that gets many feet of snow, pathway lighting might not be a viable option for you.

To install them, attach each socket to a stake and press it into your lawn. Done.

Well, almost. Be sure your male plug end is installed on the end of your pathway close to its power source.

NOTE: if you plan to outline both sides of a driveway or a sideway - places where people or vehicles may need to cross, you will want to make sure that you have a power source available on both sides of the sidewalk or driveway in order to avoid running wires across them. If you don't have power on both sides, you *must* take special care to either run the wires under the sidewalk or driveway (not likely feasible) or cover the wires with a rubber protective channel or as a last resort, stick the wires in place with a ton a gaff tape. but really, just try to avoid running wires across walkways or driveways.

Garland, Wreaths, and Bows

Wreaths and bows—oh, they love getting supersized for the holidays! It's like they're competing to be seen from space or something. But before you go all Clark Griswold with your decorations, make sure that whatever you're hanging them on can actually hold the weight. Otherwise, that loud thud you hear on Christmas Eve might not be Santa's reindeer making a stylish entrance—it could just be your decorations staging a dramatic exit.

For hanging wreaths or bows on windows, which at first seems like an impossible task, consider hanging from a nail, hook, or screw centered above your window - and use a piece of galvanized wire or something similar to tie from the hook down to your bow or wreath hanging in front of the window. Or use a widely available suction cup designed specifically for hanging Christmas decor on glass. If you go this route, make sure the suction cup is rated to hold the weight of your wreath.

For most other surfaces, wreaths and bows can be hung by using things like brick clips or, for columns, trees, railings, etc., you can secure them by wrapping a few zip ties around the columns of railing to form a temporary (seasonal) contact point, and then another zip tie around the wreath and through the zip ties wrapping around your pole/column/railing. This is my preferred method.

If your wreath or garland has lights on it, you'll need to get a little creative in how you run power to it. In most cases, you will want the male plug to end up at ground level. Once you have the wreath or garland installed, make sure to drop a short extension cord (or make one that fits perfectly!) to the ground. We'll come back later in this chapter to show you how to get everything powered up.

Bushes and Shrubs

By now, you've probably already gleaned most of my tips for installing lights on bushes and shrubs. The section about measuring bushes and lights back in the planning section covers a lot, but here are a few more tips.

If you're using light strings rather than net lights to cover your bushes and shrubs or even to wrap around the outside of smaller tree canopies, install them at the same distance apart as the spacing of the bulbs on the string itself. In other words, if you are using a light string that has bulbs spaced 4 inches apart, be sure to also install your light strings about 4 inches apart. This creates the most uniform look. You can install light strings either horizontally or vertically - make sure the spacing is nice and even and matches the spacing between the bulbs on your string as closely as possible.

If you are using net lights, be sure to install the plug ends on the same side and in the same direction so that your male plug lines up with the female plug of the previously installed net light set. Otherwise, you'll find yourself making jumpers all over your bushes to get power to everything.

Your goal should be to end up with a single male plug at the back side of your bushes and on the end closest to your power source. If your male plug is not at ground level, drop a jumper here so that your male plug ends up at or near ground level.

Tree Trunks and Canopies

Wrapping a tree canopy or trunk might look complicated from the street, but it's really just persistence at its best. Here are some tips for getting pro results.

Trunks and Trunks Wraps

Getting the best-looking trunk wrap requires only one thing. Or, rather, four things. Four fingers. We call it "the four-finger rule." For each spiral around your tree trunk (this method also applies to branches if you plan to branch wrap your tree), leave about four fingers (of an average adult hand) in width between each spiral. Holding four fingers up against your tree trunk is about how much spacing you should leave between spirals to get the best-looking result.

Make sure to start your trunk wrap a few inches off the ground and with the male plug at the bottom of the tree trunk. I recommend wrapping the string around the trunk once, then tying the male plug back onto the string itself to secure it in place. You can also use a series of zip ties to hold the bottom in place.

Slowly work your way up the tree trunk in a spiral, following the four-finger rule of spacing between your spirals. Be sure to keep the string very snug as you go.

This is especially true for brand-new light strings, which will loosen up A LOT after they are installed and have had some time to stretch out.

Once you reach your desired height, you can often tie the female end back into the string using the last spiral around the tree. If this doesn't work for you, or if your string seems very loose around the trunk, you may need to try again and pull the string tighter as you go up the trunk. You can also install a series of zip ties wrapped around the trunk every so often to keep your strings snugly in place.

Many people want to use a staple gun and slam a million staples into a tree to hold their lights in place. While this is a common practice for professional installers, it is not a technique that I recommend for beginners. If you miss and shoot a staple through a wire and don't realize it, you will have more problems than it's worth. And it will be very hard to find the culprit. Hence, I always recommend avoiding the use of staples if you can.

Branch Wraps

All the notes above will also apply if you branch-wrap your tree. But there is A LOT more to a branch wrap. For starters, you will have to do much more planning, use many more lights, and spend much more time. I mean, A LOT more time. But... the result is usually spectacular. Branch wrapping a tree is a highly detailed and time-consuming process. And, because every tree is different, there isn't a great way to explain how to properly branch-wrap a tree in words. But I'll give it a shot.

Just like you did when you measured your tree for a branch wrap back in the planning chapter, think of your tree as nothing more than a series of trunk wraps - where each branch you want to wrap is a trunk on its own. Then, wrap each branch in the same manner that you would a trunk. The difference is that you will want to stack as many male plugs as you can - i.e., as many branches as you can get onto one male plug by stacking the male plugs at the start of each branch on top of each other. The goal is to limit the number of male plugs you must jumper together when you start running power to your tree.

However you achieve it, whether it's with just a couple of male plugs or with one male plug for every branch you wrap, you will want all of the male plugs to come together such that the bottom of your tree has exactly the number of power runs that are needed to power the lights on your tree fully. What do I mean by this? Revisit Chapter 5 on Electrical Basics. If you are wrapping a large tree requiring dozens and dozens of light strings, you will want to break the power up so that you don't overland a breaker. If your tree is THAT big, then I also recommend placing it on its own dedicated electrical circuit - or more than one if it's really b ig.

I recommend breaking power runs for medium-sized trees into halves and powering each separately. And for large trees, I usually separate them into quadrants or even eighths. Your tree will be unique, and I won't be able to provide precise guidance in this book. Just be sure to measure how much power your tree lights are using, break your power runs up accordingly, and run as many separate power runs from as many dedicated circuits as required to power your tree safely.

NOTE: If you're scratching your head over this whole branch wrap ordeal, it might be time to call in the pros (see Chapter 11). Or, you could just play it safe and go with a classy trunk wrap. Either way, your trees will thank you—and maybe even high-five you if they had hands!

Canopy Wraps

Wrapping a tree canopy with lights is easier, less expensive, and less time-consuming than branch-wrapping a tree. But it will still take some time and effort. Here are a few tips to get you started.

Just like everything else in your display, you will want the male plugs to end up at the bottom. In the case of tree canopies, you will want your male plug to end up near the center top of your trunk, right where the canopy of your tree begins. So that's where I recommend you start. Secure the male plug of the first string of your canopy wrap to a spot at the top of your tree trunk. Then, swag the light string out to the perimeter of your canopy. Or wrap it around a lower branch to get it to the outer canopy.

There are many ways to wrap lights around a tree canopy - and they are all correct. So you can just experiment until you find the look you like best. Lots of folks wrap the light strings around the canopy in a spiral pattern all the way to the top. Others like to go up and over and back and forth. And some prefer a very random look. All that matters is that you are happy with how it looks when you light it up!

> > > > > **PRO TIP** < < < < <

When wrapping light strings around the outside of a tree canopy, don't just plug them together end-to-end. If you do, they will easily come unplugged when the wind blows. And that will be a difficult fix. Instead, when you come to the end of a string of lights, take the female and tie it together (literally, like you are tying a shoelace) to the male end of the next string of lights. This way, they will stay plugged in when the wind blows.

For most trees, even smaller ones, wrapping around a tree canopy will require some way to reach to the very top of your tree. This is where having an extension pole comes in handy. Sometimes an extension pole AND a ladder are needed in order to reach the top. And for big trees, you may even need to rent a cherry picker. In fact, if you can afford to rent a cherry picker (see Chapter 3), I highly recommend doing so.

I won't cover using a cherry picker here, but if your tree is less than 20 feet to the top, you can find an extension pole that will allow you to reach high enough to install your lights. It will take dozens of walks around your tree, but with patience, it will be done in no time. And your family and neighbors will love you for it! You'll probably be a little dizzy! But it will be gorgeous!

Once you have your canopy lights installed, you'll want to drop an extension cord (or jumper) from the male plug (or plugs) that now sit up in your canopy or at the top of your trunk and drop the male plug end closer to the ground for getting it powered up (more on that later).

Lastly, use a few zip ties strung together and wrap around your tree trunk in a couple of spots to hold your extension cord/jumper in place for the holiday season.

Wireframe Displays, Inflatables, Blow Molds, Wood Cut-Outs, and Other Types of Yard Decor

Installation is usually pretty simple for most other types of yard decor. Place the decor where it looks the most awesome, and run an extension cord to it if it needs power. That's about it! Done!

Sort of. There are a couple of things to consider when it comes to stand-alone displays and decorations. Each piece must be secured exceptionally well to the ground. I always recommend using a guy wire system (see Chapter 3) to secure any display piece that stands more than 8 feet tall. Sometimes, smaller pieces require guy wiring as well. The largest inflatables will come with a guy wiring system. But for any DIY display pieces you build, you will have to be the judge of whether or not it needs to be guy-wired.

Wireframe displays that are under about 4-6 feet tall will usually already have built-in ground stakes, but if they don't, or your wireframe displays are taller or you made them yourself and they don't have deep ground stakes, I always advise adding a guy wire system to secure these pieces as well.

When it comes to blow molds and other smaller, lightweight decorations, there aren't really any great ways to secure them in place. So you'll have to play it by ear. I've seen some creative ways of securing smaller display pieces. Use your new-found holiday hero skill set to create something unique and fabulous!

>>>>> **PRO TIP** <<<<<

DO NOT UNDERESTIMATE THE POWER OF MOTHER NATURE! "The bigger they are, the harder they fall" is never truer than for large decorations. Make sure everything is guy-wired and securely anchored to the ground.

Powering Your Display

This is the big one—your final hurdle on the track to becoming a holiday hero: preparing to flip the switch! This step is crucial because if you mess up, you'll end up with a dud display, tripping breakers, or, heaven forbid, a full-blown bonfire. Yep, for real. Let's dive into how to avoid turning your grand light show into a grand disaster.

Every display is different, every home is different, and every decorator has a different skill level when installing a Christmas display for the first time. I won't be able to address every possible scenario in this book. But I can guide you on how to ensure you get your grand vision wired up correctly and safely.

First things first. With a freshly caffeinated brain and a focus on attention to detail, walk through your grand masterpiece of a display and remind yourself of the locations of every male plug that needs power.

Look for clusters of decor that can be plugged in together. For example, if you have four windows across the left front of your house and some lit garland around your front door - create an extension cord using SPT wire like this:

1. Install a female slide-on plug on the end of your uncut roll of wire and plug Window 1 into this female plug.

2. Unroll your wire until you have enough length to drop from window 1 to the ground, over to window 2, and up to your male plug on window 2
.

3. Install an inline female plug at this position, and plug window 2 into this female inline plug.

4. Continue unrolling your bulk SPT wire back down to the ground, over to window 3, and up to the male plug on window 3.

5. Install an inline female plug at this position, and plug window 3 into this female inline plug.

6. Continue unrolling your bulk SPT wire back down to the ground, over to window 4, and up to the male plug on window 4.

7. Install an inline female plug at this position, and plug window 4 into this female inline plug.

8. Continue unrolling your bulk SPT wire back down to the ground, over to your door garland, and up to the male plug on your garland.

9. Install an inline female plug at this position, and plug your door garland

into this female inline plug.

10. Now, unroll enough of your bulk SPT wire to reach your power source. Make sure to leave enough slack to neatly tuck away and hide the wire wherever you can. Once you have the right length, cut the wire from the spool and install a male slide-on plug at the end of the wire.

11. Plug it in! Now, you have all four windows and your door garland on a single extension cord perfectly cut to fit your display. Beautiful!

>>>>> **PRO TIP** <<<<<

Plug Stacking. Almost all standard Christmas light strings have stackable male plugs (see Chapter 3). This means they have a male plug on one side of the plug and a female plug on the other. It also means that you can plug the male end of a light string into the female back side of another string right at the source of power. This comes in REALLY handy for managing power distribution throughout your display. I always recommend stacking plugs everywhere you can throughout your display. It will make wiring things up a lot easier.

You can use this same approach to prepare power for your entire display. Here are some guidelines:

- Think of your display as if it were in sections: roof outline, roof fascia, each window or bank of windows, left side bushes, right side bushes, left yard decor, right yard decor, each tree individually, etc. Then, group your lit decor together in the same manner I describe above.

- Make sure you know how much power each section or prop within your display requires. Use a tool like the Kil-A-Watt to measure how much power each section is pulling.

- Create a drawing showing the amperage requirements (based on the measurements you just took) and use this to determine which items can all be plugged in together on the same power run.

- Use inline female plugs or 3-way triple taps to reduce the number of separate male plugs to just 1 or 2 for male plugs at each of your power sources, never exceeding about 12 amps on a 15-amp circuit.

- Some homes have a walkway right up the middle. Try to avoid running wires across walkways and driveways. If you have walkways or a driveway separating sections of your display, use a power source on each side to avoid running wires over walkways or your driveway.

- Be sure to measure the power load and not overload your breaker. I recommend staying under 12 amps total per circuit. And always make sure that you are never pulling more than 6 amps through any single section of SPT wire. This is a conservative, safe way to run your power.

It will take a little time and some math, but once you have it figured out - and documented on your display drawings - it will be much easier and faster to install next year.

> >>>>> **PRO TIP** <<<<<
>
> *Make sure that plugs are not sitting in a location that will become a puddle if it rains or your sprinkler system gets a little carried away. Use a zip tie to hold your plugs and electrical connections up off the ground by tying them to the back of a lower branch on a bush, up a few inches on a tree trunk or post, etc., as needed.*

Installing and Setting Up Your Timer

Although using a timer isn't required, I always recommend them. It just makes things easy. If your display consists of only roof lights, for example, it may be just as easy to plug them in and unplug them each evening.

If your display has many elements and uses multiple outlets, it will be worth your time and money to invest in enough timers to control every outlet. I covered the details of different types of timers back in Chapter 3, but here they are again for your easy reference:

- **Manual Timers:** These are the most basic of timers; you simply plug your lights into them and manually set the on/off times using a dial or switch.

- **Digital Timers:** These are more advanced than manual timers, as they allow for more precise scheduling and often have additional features

- **Smart Timers:** These high-tech gadgets connect to your phone and allow for remote control of your lights, as well as more advanced scheduling options and smart home integration.

- **Photocell Timers:** These timers use a light sensor to automatically turn on your lights at dusk and off at dawn, making them perfect for outdoor displays. Just make sure you place the sensor in an area that gets enough light during the day.

- **Programmable Timers:** These timers allow you to set different schedules for each day of the week, making them great for those who like to mix it up with their lighting displays.

- **Advanced Timers and Control:** If you want to get really fancy with our display, try using something like the GFade 8 controller available at thechristmaslightemporium.com. The GFade allows you to not only schedule your lights to turn on and off in whatever way you want them to - including different times for every day or even multiple different times every day, but it also allows you to program the lights to turn on with a ramp up/fade, along with lots of other cool tricks. It will pretty much allow you to do anything you want with your lights.

Viola! Your Christmas extravaganza is now installed and ready to power up for the first time! WHOOOP! Fire that baby up!

Chapter Eleven

When to Hire a Professional

Ah, the holiday season! That magical time when the air gets brisker, stores get jollier, and homes shine brighter than a disco ball.

But how do you get that disco ball glow if you're afraid of heights? Or you don't know much about electricity. Or maybe you're busier than Santa's Elves and don't have the time to install your vision of a Christmas-themed Studio 54! These are all good reasons why some folks ask themselves, 'Do I need a pro installer?"

If you're thinking, "I don't have the time or skills, or time to learn the skills—**BUT I STILL WANT THE BRIGHTEST HOUSE IN THE CITY!**" then this chapter is for you.

While you may feel like you may lose a little 'hero' status with those who may be judging your hero meter, calling in a pro to sprinkle those festive sparks could be the savviest move you make this holiday season. Seriously, let's chat about why outsourcing your outdoor Christmas decorating might buy you more time and make your holidays safer, shinier, and more dazzling than that one time Uncle Bob tried to make eggnog. Trust me, it'll be a bright decision!

Why Hire a Professional Christmas Light Installer?

Professional Christmas light installers offer unmatched value. Not only do they enhance the aesthetic appeal of your outdoor spaces, but they also save you from the hassle of untangling lights and dealing with potential hazards. They ensure your lights remain functional throughout the season by providing maintenance services and troubleshooting any technical issues that arise. In short, they save you a TON of time, and they have the experience to do a better job of turning your front yard into a Studio 54-style Christmas Wonderland.

- **Safety First:** Climbing ladders and roofs during the icy months poses a significant safety risk. Professionals are trained to install lights efficiently and without injury, providing you with peace of mind.

- **Time Efficiency:** Your time is valuable, especially during the busy holiday season. Professionals handle the complex and time-consuming planning and installation process quickly and efficiently.

- **Spectacular Results:** With their experience, pros can turn your home into a festive wonderland with pristine light designs and layouts that you might not achieve on your own.

Rule #1: Cheaper is not better. *Do not base your decision on the lowest cost. Base it on which company is the best fit for your project.*

There's always a guy in the neighborhood, isn't there? He can fix your sink, your toilet, your fridge, your fence, your light fixtures, change your tires, help your kid understand the moral complications of "The Scarlet Letter," mow your lawn, and, of course, put up your Christmas lights "cheaper than anybody else." Don't fall for it. Just ask around. You'll hear tons of stories about wires catching fire, installations not being completed, the guy not showing up when he said he would, or at all - and countless other stories. These are the types of experiences you can expect if you skimp when hiring a Christmas light installer who is *not* a Professional Christmas Light Installer.

Nothing against the handyman and the general contractor; they have saved my butt on numerous occasions when I've put uncooked beans down the garbage disposal or failed to notice the dog gnawing a 4-foot hole in the fence. However, if installing your Christmas lights is proving to be beyond your capability, there's a good chance the guy who mows your lawn or walks your dog isn't *really* going to know any more than you do about how to bring your Christmas vision to life.

That's when it might be time to call in a Professional Christmas Light Installer.

But remember, there's a reason they are called "Professional Christmas Light Installers." Simply put: experience. Not to mention full-time crews of skilled installers, insurance in case anything goes wrong with their installation, guarantees on their work, and access to the highest quality, professional-grade Christmas lights and decorations that money can buy. It's all they do. And they're the best at it.

Key Experience and Skills to Look For

When considering a professional installer, look for individuals or companies with extensive experience, well-honed technical skills, and a creative flair. They should have knowledge of electrical systems and expertise in safe and effective installation techniques. Exceptional customer service, prompt response times, and a portfolio showcasing past work are excellent indicators of a competent professional.

Essential Questions to Ask

1. What is your experience with Christmas light installations?

2. Can I see examples of your previous work?

3. Do you have references I can call?

4. Do you offer both installation and removal services?

5. Who owns and stores the lights, me or you? (i.e., am I leasing or buying?)

6. Do you have experience installing my type/style/size of display?

7. What safety precautions do you take during installation?

8. Are you insured and licensed?

9. What is the timeline for installation and post-holiday take-down?

CLIPA Certified Installers

One surefire thing to ask is if the company or professional you're hiring is CLIPA[1] Certified. CLIPA is the Christmas Light Installation Pros Association. It was started in 2017 as a Facebook group and has grown to include contractors, distributors, and vendors from all over the US and Canada. It offers training classes and certifications that are not mandatory to install lights but confer a degree of ability and commitment to excellence.

The Christmas Light Installation Professionals Association (CLIPA) sets the gold standard in the industry. Founded to foster excellence and reliability among Christmas light installers, CLIPA offers certification programs that equip installers with the best practices, latest technology updates, and safety protocols. Hiring a CLIPA-certified installer gives you direct access to industry experts com-

---

1. https://clipau.com/

mitted to delivering elite-level services, ensuring your home glows with joyous perfection.

> "The mission of CLIPA is to better our industry and provide consumers with a network of Christmas Light Installation Professionals that are properly trained and qualified to make certain that their customer satisfaction level is as high as possible."
>
> Matt Hyden, Managing Partner, CLIPA

You can find a list of CLIPA Certified Installers on their website here: https://clipa.com/directory/

> >>>>> **PRO TIP** <<<<<
>
> *Putting lights on the roof and the trees is the wheelhouse of most Professional Christmas Light Installation Companies. Dazzling light shows that jump, dance, and incorporate a hologram Santa and a custom musical soundtrack are usually not something they can do. If you are looking for someone to design your display, program a computer-controlled synchronized light show, or install a display with so much high-tech wizardry that even the most skilled computer scientist would be flustered - then you don't need a professional Christmas light installer. Rather, you need a specialized holiday production services company. If this is the case for you, I recommend Extreme Lightscapes (extremelightscapes.com).*

Picture this: you're staring at a tangled mess of Christmas lights, and it dawns on you—why not let a pro handle this festive fiasco? Hiring a professional Christmas light installer is as brilliant a choice as the twinkling lights themselves. Trust me, it's a gift that keeps on giving—enhancing your home's holiday spirit while freeing up precious time to focus on what really matters: avoiding Aunt Edna's fruitcake and actually enjoying your time with family!

It's More Than Just a Business

I reached out to Lidsay Lights and Alex Bush, the co-owners of Light Up Your Life Holiday Lights, based in Davison, Michigan. I asked them to share with you, dear Memory Maker, what Christmas means to them and why they enjoy helping their customers create the smiles, memories, and joy that ultimately create more hope in the world.

We love Christmas because it fills the world with magic and generosity. It reminds us of the ultimate good in the world and brings families together. Christmas also means that it's Jesus's birthday, and we celebrate the day an awesome person was born.

A homeowner might consider a professional light installer to ensure their safety and have a display that looks perfect! There are lots of reasons to hire a pro! One - products! Professional lights are of the highest quality. Two - safety. Three - don't deal with tangled cords or burned-out bulbs. Fourth - stay out of the cold. Fifth - the logistics and calculations of running power to all your display elements. Six - why wouldn't you!

If you're considering hiring a professional installer, look at their previous work and Christmas spirit! Look for great Google reviews! Don't give your money to someone you are not confident in. There are endless horror stories of people whose light installer didn't come back for takedown or didn't answer the phone the following year, but they have all your lights! Call early—even in

July! You'll want to ensure the installer is insured and has the necessary certifications.

We are *Light up your Life - Holiday Lights*. Ran by a boyfriend-girlfriend team - we shine light in dark places. We are part of the mission to help people experience moments of magic! We want to help light it up! There is too much darkness in the world. We know beautiful twinkling and shining lights bring a positive feeling to everyone! Lights also have a unique ability to gather a bunch of attention! These two things combined are a superpower for spreading positivity, joy, and hope! It's our mission to share that with the entire universe.

Thank you for the opportunity to share!
Alex Bush and Lindsay Lights, Light Up Your Life Holiday Lights

If you'd like to learn more about Alex and Lindsay and their company, Light Up Your Life Holiday Lights, you can check them out here:
https://www.atbconstructionservices.com/holiday-and-event-lighting

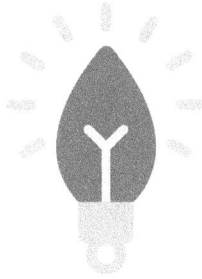

Chapter Twelve

Maintenance and Troubleshooting

There has never been a yard in the history of Christmas that didn't have technical glitches. If you want to tell me about this one time yours was flawless back in 1999, I know you're lying. There are always going to be problems. Yet, with a quick checklist of common issues and some detective work, you can quickly solve most issues and bring the magic back to your yard!

For most modern displays, you will be using LED bulbs and strings, so I will focus on them here. However, many of these troubleshooting tips will also apply to incandescent bulbs and strings.

IMPORTANT: Always unplug your lights before working on any type of repair!

Here are some of the most common issues and how to deal with them:

1. **Fuses:** Fuses are a vital component of your light strings, designed to

prevent electrical overloads that can lead to fires. A top reason fuses blow is overly ambitious connections—when too many strings are connected end-to-end or you're using more power than the breaker can handle.

They go out a lot and are designed so that if one goes out, everything past it will, too. That seems really annoying until you remember the whole thing about how an out-of-control fire could destroy everything you own.

Replacing a blown fuse is simple: locate the fuse compartment on the male end of the plug, often accessible with a small screwdriver. Slide it open, replace the faulty fuse, and be sure to stock up on spares to minimize downtime.

Also, note that most slide-on plugs do not contain fuses. Just as store-bought extension cords usually don't contain fuses. But just about every pre-made string of lights out there that is UL-listed will have a fuse inside the male plug.

2. **Non-Working C7 or C9 Sockets**: usually, moisture is the culprit; invest in socket stuffers to cover unused sockets that don't have bulbs screwed into them, and use o-rings to help keep moisture out, especially if your bulbs are installed pointing straight up. If a bulb won't light up in one socket but it does in another socket, check the socket. Make sure the pin in the bottom of the socket is touching the bottom of the bulb firmly and that the metal pin running up the inside wall of the socket is making a solid connection with the threaded side of the bulb. Make sure the socket actually *has* both a bottom pin AND a side pin - sometimes, these pieces get left out at the factory!

If you find a completely broken socket that is not usable, you can always grab a pack of replacement sockets from The Christmas Light Emporium, pop the broken one-off, and install a new one using your handy C Clamp (see chapter 3!)

3. **Misbehaving LED String Lights:** LED strings are typically very durable, but they can still hit snags—the main culprits being blown fuses, incorrect polarity, or damaged rectifiers. Enter the LED Keeper tool and pods - available at The Christmas Light Emporium, of course! These gadgets are your best friends for testing and repairing defective LED light strings. Should the entire string show no signs of life even after testing and repair attempts using an LED Keeper, a damaged rectifier may be to blame, necessitating a complete replacement. Even if your light string says, "If one bulb goes out, the rest stay lit!" a bad rectifier will still cause problems. If you have an LED string with a rectifier in the middle of the string (most do), and you find that half of the string won't light up - this is almost always a sign of a bad rectifier, and you will need to replace the string.

4. **Tracking Down Electrical Shorts/Tripped Breakers**: GFCI breakers are hyper-vigilant watchdogs, frequently tripping when they detect moisture, staples piercing strings, or defective breakers. If your display goes dark during a damp spell, rest assured the GFCI is protecting your home. Investigating involves checking for pinched wires and water exposure and establishing where exactly the trip occurred in your display. The most common culprits are moisture, too many lights on a single outlet, and staples piercing through a wire.

If you have lights lying directly on the ground, you can expect your outdoor GFCI breaker to stay tripped until they dry out. They will trip faster than lights not on the ground due to power leaks on a grounded circuit. It just means your GFCI is doing its job.

5. **Lights are Dimmer at the Far End of a Run:** Dim lights at the far end of a long run of light bulbs or strings could indicate a power drop over its length, particularly in *Really* long runs. A voltage meter will come in handy to diagnose this. Consider using heavier gauge wires to mitigate the drop or opt for shorter string segments to maintain even brightness throughout. Revisit Chapter 5 for more details about voltage drop over distance.

6. **Lights Will Not Turn on When Plugged In**: If specific sections, strings, or props in your display refuse to light up, first inspect slide-on plugs for misalignment or bent teeth. Confirm all components are snugly connected and revisit all wiring for possible oversight. These meticulous checks are often the key to restoring sparkle. I hate to say it, but also make sure they are actually plugged into a live power source!

7. **Critters Chewing on Wires:** It's astounding how enticing Christmas lights are to wildlife. Animals, particularly rodents, love to chew on wires, causing chaos. Shield your wires and decorations with protective coverings if you can, and if you have a critter problem, consider using repellents to dissuade them from turning your display into their personal snack bar.

Keeping your Christmas lights shining bright might feel like wrestling a tangle of holiday chaos, but the tips above will have you troubleshooting like a pro in no time. And you'll be swapping fuses with the finesse of a seasoned electrician and outsmarting those sneaky critters that see your lights as a tasty snack!

Chapter Thirteen

Take Down and Storage

Christmas lights and decorations are a long-term investment that you would ideally like to last for a decade or more, considering the time, money, and effort you've put into them. Taking the time to clean your items and make sure they are really well maintained is just common sense, but that doesn't mean we do it every time, do we? Yes, we do. Here are some general pointers that will ensure your products and equipment last for a long time and that you will have a much easier time getting your setup together for next Christmas.

IMPORTANT: Before You Take Anything Down

Draw a sketch and take photos of your display. Add the details of your *actual* installation to the sketches/drawings you made during the planning stage. Include notes about where you ran electrical and which lights and decorations were installed where and take pictures of everything!

Reverse Engineering

Removing your holiday extravaganza will take a lot less time than installing it—typically about 1/10th the amount of time. Think of it as reverse engineering. Take one aspect of your display at a time and simply reverse your installation process—slowly, safely, and patiently.

Clean, Inspect, and Repair As You Take Things Down

Your lights and decor have now been outside for several weeks and, in most of the country, have been subject to rain, snow, ice, hail, sleet, or heat. When you're cleaning each item, look for any cracks, tears, breaks, fissures, or anything else that looks like it might be a future problem. If you find problems, fix them now. That way, everything will be ready to go when you pull it out of storage for next year.

Take Things Down Carefully

When I was younger, my mom once walked on me unplugging the vacuum cleaner Indiana Jones style, which means grabbing it at its source on the unit and whipping it out of the wall from maybe 20 feet away. My reward for this sweet move was to vacuum the carpet three times a week after school for the rest of my adolescence. Please don't pull the lights down with any sort of hard tugging. You're either going to rip them apart or leave big holes behind where they were attached to your brand-new brick or put yourself in the hospital. An equally big warning is to make sure everything is powered off and disconnected. Electricity likes going through the insulated cables, but has no problem going through your not-so-insulated body too. Take your time, especially with difficult props and lights that are in high places like your roof and trees. This isn't a rush job. It will take a lot of little moves of the ladder as you get it all done. Never lean or try to stand on one foot or decide to go full Tarzan in order to get them down faster. It's not worth the risk to you or the lights.

Pay special attention to the trickier parts that could damage your property if you aren't careful. Things like clips glued/screwed to trim/brick can cause a lot of damage if you don't take your time when removing them. If you do end up with a bit of damage, well, what's one more home repair project added to the list, right?

Label everything

My wife has four big bins of Christmas stuff inside the house. They all are the same color, shape, and size, and they all say "CHRISTMAS" on them. Never once in two decades have we found the right thing out of the right container on the first try. You can do better. You can color code the lights or just be really descriptive about what is in each container so you're not wasting time sorting it out next year. A really smart idea is to take photos of your display for reference if you're planning on doing the same design next year. You can even make a collage of the entire process, print out the photos, and attach them to the underside of the container's lid so it's right where you need it to be next year.

If you have a large display, you should consider making and inventory list with Google Sheets or Excel. Number every tub and list those numbers in a spreadsheet indicating the contents of every tub. It will come in handy, I promise.

Label your extension cords, especially if you made them to custom fit your display. Roll them up and use a piece of white electrical tape and a Sharpie to label each cord or bundle of cords with the name of the prop it goes with and a number. Then, jot that number down on your drawing for each reference. If you have started a spreadsheet to track everything, add it to that spreadsheet. There is no such thing as over-preparing for next year.

Ball Your Lights

When taking down light strings, roll them into balls, not into donuts or wheels or any other shape. Getting lights wrapped the wrong way and having to spend the first few hours of next year's labor process unrolling and untangling them is one of the most frustrating experiences you can force yourself to go through. Make sure you always roll up your lights starting with the female end in your hand, so that the male end ends up on the outside of the ball. This makes it easy to pull out your lights and use them next year without having to untangle them. For roof lines (C7/(socket wire/light line) roll up like you would an extension cord and use a couple of zip ties to hold the bundle together in at least 2-3 spots.

Storage Options for Different Types of Decor

When it comes to storage options for different types of Christmas lights and decorations, there are endless options. From pre-fab containers to DIY solutions, covering and protecting your display components will make all the difference in preserving your holiday treasures and setting you up for a seamless setup next year!

For light strings, consider using storage reels or spools designed specifically for string lights. These tools prevent tangling and make it easy to unwind them without the same ol' hassle. An alternative is rolling the lights into balls, as mentioned before, to keep them tidy and untangled. For wreaths and garlands, invest in durable storage bags or bins. Some even come with handles or hanging hooks for easy access and protective covers to keep them dust-free and in stellar condition.

For larger decorations like blow molds, wood cutouts, and oversized ornaments, large, clear storage boxes or REALLY big, clear trash bags can work great. Durable and spacious, they allow visibility into the contents, making it a breeze to find what you need without rummaging. Stackable bins maximize your storage space without sacrificing accessibility.

Meanwhile, delicate decorations should be stored in padded containers with dividers to separate and protect each piece. Collapsible crates can be handy for those larger, more awkward decorations that don't benefit from being stacked on top of one another up.

From the lit-up pathways across your lawn to majestic tree toppers, ensuring every piece has its own spot to rest until next year can transform your holiday setup from chaotic to cheerful! Plus, labeling each bin with its contents takes the guesswork out of decorating next season.

Find a Dry, Cool, Critter-Free Spot to Store Everything

Be aware of temperature limitations on any of your decor so you don't get it out next year to find a slab of rusted metal, melted plastic, or a pile of broken glass. Make sure your storage containers don't have cracks or broken tops. Pests can and will chew on anything. If it gets too hot in the summer where you live, find a spot in the basement or the spare room to keep everything safe.

Keep everything well protected, and it will last for many years. Store your display in a temperature and humidity-controlled location if you can, as it is always a better option, especially if you live in a hot summer climate, etc.

Chapter Fourteen

Pro Tips Recap

PRO TIP: All of the principles I share in this book will apply if you ever venture into the wild world of synchronized Christmas light shows. You will still have to learn everything I mention in this book—and more.

PRO TIP: If you are interested in exploring the world of synchronized music and light shows, start early. Give yourself at least a full year to learn the ropes. It's a lot.

PRO TIP: Always plug your lights into GFCI-protected outlets when used outdoors. GFCI-protected outlets are designed to watch for strange behavior in the electrical flow. If they detect anything unusual, they will immediately trip your breaker - keeping everyone safe. The electrical code requires all outdoor electrical outlets to be GFCI-protected. But don't be surprised! You can expect your lights not to work when it is raining or wet, and there is a power leak, or if you accidentally drive a staple into a light string. This is OKAY! It just means your GFCI circuits are doing their job. Once everything dries out, you can reset your breaker, and your glorious display will return to life.

BONUS TIP: Most homes have outdoor GFCI outlets running on a 15-amp breaker. Always keep your maximum load under 12 amps (80%).

PRO TIP: Use a "Kill A Watt" Device to Measure Amps and Voltage. It's much easier and safer to use than a multimeter. You can find them on Amazon and other online shops. I recommend it for new decorators and anyone who wants a simpler, safer, easier way to measure and manage the power behind their magnificent Christmas display.

PRO TIP: When measuring your roof, bushes, driveway, or anything else to determine how much lighting, garland, or other material you will need, always round up or add 10-20% to avoid any "Oops, I'm short" moments.

PRO TIP: When hanging garland around a door or window, you can add a little more of a pro touch by slightly swagging the top. By adding a nail or screw on the left corner and another at the right corner that is parallel and then adding a third screw at the center above your door about 2-4 inches higher than the corners, you can allow the garland or lights to slightly swag, creating a really professional look. Some folks even like to add some mistletoe or a bow at the high center point of the swag for even more pizzazz!

PRO TIP: Pro installers almost always use 6-inch-spaced C7 bulbs and strings to outline doors and windows while using 12-inch-spaced C9 bulbs to outline roof fascia and peaks.

PRO TIP: When wrapping trees, always make sure to start with your male plug at the bottom of the tree. The last thing you want is a male plug 15 feet up in a tree and having to run power to it.

PRO TIP: The most common type, length, and spacing of light strings that professional installers use for wrapping trees are 5mm LED strings with 70 bulbs with 4-inch spacing or 5mm LED strings with 50 bulbs and 6-inch spacing. The most elegant displays will always use 70-bulb strings with 4-inch spacing. However, 50-bulb strings with 6-inch spacing will cost less, so if you are budget-conscious, this may be a good option for you.

PRO TIP: If you are planning to wrap the exterior canopy of a tree and measure the tree wraps for your display during the spring, summer, or fall months, be sure to consider the TYPE of the tree you are planning to wrap. Many types of trees have dense foliage in the summer/fall but lose their leaves in the fall/winter. Sometimes, this doesn't leave you with anything much to attach lights to! Always imagine your tree canopy without any leaves and plan your canopy wrapping around bare branches only.

PRO TIP: Experiment with using larger bulbs in the canopies of your trees. Some of the most elegant canopy wraps you see use C9 bulbs and strings - the same type you find outlining most rooflines - rather than a smaller standard light string. Draping them over and around a tree canopy can be an exquisite look for mid-size to large trees. Also, consider using a different light color in the canopy than you use on your trunk wraps. For example, a warm white for your trunk wrap and vibrant red C9 bulbs draped around the exterior of your canopy.

PRO TIP: If you decide to go all out and branch-wrap your outdoor tree but need to keep the budget and time requirement in check, skip some of the mid-size and smaller branches that form the canopy of a tree. By focusing only on the major branches in your tree canopy (usually the widest and longest branches), you can shave 50% off the time and cost of a fully branch-wrapped tree. And no one will notice the unwrapped smaller branches.

PRO TIP: To determine how many light strings you need for a pine tree (indoor or outdoor), hop on over to The Christmas Light Emporium website and use Rudolph's Christmas Tree Light String Calculator! It will provide you with the number of strings you need for your pine tree with no math required! It will calculate the number of strings you need for each type of light string and any pine tree with a canopy base up to 15 feet wide and a canopy height up to 30 feet.

PRO TIP: *NEVER INSTALL A MALE PLUG ON BOTH ENDS OF A PIECE OF WIRE OR SOCKET STRINGER!!!!! We call this a 'suicide string'. If you do this and you, or one of your helpers, decide to plug one end into a hot electrical source, you will then have two hot metal prongs on the other end. This could lead to serious consequences, including electrical shock, severe injuries, or fire. Don't do this ever, for any reason.*

PRO TIP: NEVER plug a coiled electrical product directly into a power source without unrolling it and cutting off the length you need! Coiled bulk wire products like SPT1, rope light, etc., will create high levels of resistance if left coiled AND plugged into a power source. This can lead to melting and fire. Trust me. I've seen it happen more than once.

PRO TIP: The best tool to push the bottom cap onto a C7 or C9 replacement socket is a vise grip C-Clamp. These have flat plates that swivel, allowing them to lock the bottom cap in place evenly and quickly with much less effort than trying to push the bottom cap on with your bare hands.

PRO TIP: Don't wrap your electrical connections with electrical tape. If you do, moisture created by condensation or leakage will likely get inside the connection. The only way to dry them out will be to remove the tape and let them dry out. It's also a pain if you have other troubleshooting issues to resolve, like needing to replace a light string that has been taped together with other strings in an end-to-end connection. Pro installers don't wrap electrical connections with electrical tape, and neither should you.

PRO TIP: Pay attention to the maximum weight rating from your ladder manufacturer. This is important. I'm a big guy, and I work with a lot of big guys. We need beefy ladders. You don't want your ladder collapsing while trying to spread your holiday cheer - or ever!

PRO TIP: Remember that the best light is the one that brings you joy (and maybe a little bit of eye-rolling from your neighbors).

PRO TIP: Use flood lights to add that 'pro' look to your outdoor trees. Even if you wrap your trees with light strings, adding the same color flood light pointing from the ground and up onto your tree will add a massive touch of elegance and really make them pop!

PRO TIP: To power a lit wreath hanging in the middle of a door, make sure the wire is long enough to let the door swing all the way open – preferably, use dark wire for a dark door or white or light color for a light color door. This way, the door will retain its full ability to swing open while remaining as 'invisible' as possible. I recommend running a separate extension cord for your wreaths. Run the extension cord up one side of your doorway and swag the power down from the top corner of the hinged side of the door.

BONUS TIP: Installing a garland around your door will provide a nice place to hide the extension cord that powers your door wreath.

PRO TIP: Pros and Cons of Hot Glue and Staples – Hot glue offers a quick and strong adhesion for affixing lights to surfaces such as wood or brick. For this reason, it is a popular technique. But the downside of using hot glue is that it will almost always leave some damage behind when you take the lights down. Staples are also popular for securing light strings to wood surfaces. It is fast and offers a secure installation option. But, like hot glue (or even screwing in a C-Clip), it will leave some damage behind in the form of small holes that will have to be repaired at some point.

PRO TIP: When wrapping light strings around the outside of a tree canopy, don't just plug them together end-to-end. If you do, they will easily come unplugged when the wind blows. And that will be a difficult fix. Instead, when you come to the end of a string of lights, take the female and tie it together (literally, like you are tying a shoelace) to the male end of the next string of lights. This way, they will stay plugged in when the wind blows.

PRO TIP: DO NOT UNDERESTIMATE THE POWER OF MOTHER NATURE! "The bigger they are, the harder they fall" is never truer than for large decorations. Make sure everything is guy-wired and securely anchored to the ground.

PRO TIP: Plug Stacking. Almost all standard Christmas light strings have stackable male plugs (see Chapter 3). This means they have a male plug on one side of the plug and a female plug on the other. It also means you can plug the male end of a light string into the female back side of another string right at the source of power. This comes in REALLY handy for managing power distribution throughout your display. I always recommend stacking plugs everywhere you can throughout your display. It will make wiring things up a lot easier.

PRO TIP: Make sure that plugs are not sitting in a location that will become a puddle if it rains or your sprinkler system gets a little carried away. Use a zip tie to hold your plugs and electrical connections up off the ground by tying them to the back of a lower branch on a bush, up a few inches on a tree trunk or post, etc., as needed.

PRO TIP: Roll your light strings into balls. Be sure to start with the female plug end so that the male end is on the outside of your balled string. Roll them into a ball. Not a doughnut. Doughnuts are bad for you. Doughnuts. Bad. This will make installation of your lights much easier. Roll them back up the same way when you take them down. It makes storage and maintenance much easier.

PRO TIP: Tape drawings and photos onto the inside lid of your storage boxes and store 'prop' components together in the same tub. If a component of your display requires more than one tub for storage, clearly label them on the outside as 1 of 3, 2 or 3, 3 of 3, etc.

Conclusion

I've covered an enormous amount of territory throughout the previous 14 chapters while you've learned a few fancy new words and hopefully had a few laughs. This is a book you can revisit time and again for helpful pointers, honest advice, and encouragement on how to put together a remarkable Christmas display like a pro – one that will make your neighbors green with envy and turn you into a holiday hero!

I want to reiterate three points above all to ensure that you get the most out of your quest to create the ultimate Christmas spectacle with your DIY outdoor Christmas decorating.

1. **Stay safe.** You are working with things that are sometimes hot, usually electrified (a whole different type of hot!), and you risk creating significant damage if you are unprepared. It's not just your safety I'm concerned about, but your family's, the people who live around you, the people who come check out your display, and nearby houses, trees, and other structures that you are temporarily converting into a winter wonderland.

My rule is that if I don't know how something works, I do my research, learn the tools and techniques for the task, and prepare for a successful installation, no matter how much time it may take - instead of diving in headfirst and hoping for the best. When installing lights and decor, I highly recommend you wear close-toed shoes or work boots, long pants, a long-sleeve shirt, work gloves, and even a hard hat if you're working in a tree or on the roof. It's better to over-prepare than to go out there dressed like you're going to the lake for the weekend - and wind up in the ER instead.

2. **Plan early and plan often.** If you like fables, you want to be the Ant, who is constantly getting ready for the long winter by storing food, not the Grasshopper, who apparently has some short-term memory issue and is out there hitting the club, eating Taco Bell at 3 a.m., and thinking summer will last forever.

The more you plan things on paper, a spreadsheet, and so on, the less likely you are to make mistakes, the less likely you are to go over budget, and the more likely you are to get your lights and decor installed with minimal pain and suffering. The gratification of having a line of cars outside your house to see your magnificent creation is amazing. To reach this pinnacle of decorating achievement - becoming a holiday hero - the planning and installation process must be a positive experience, not something you dread every holiday season.

3. **Share the joy and hope of the season.** Christmas is not my favorite time of year simply because of the lights and decorations. It's the season where love takes over. We remember why we're all here, and we celebrate with joy and happiness. We take the time to embrace not only friends

and family but also neighbors, coworkers, and people we might have seen 100 times and never spoken to.

Like most people, my attitude towards Christmas has changed over time. It started with me as a child wondering what the heck Santa's problem was when I asked for 13 things on my list and only got 7, it changed dramatically when I had kids and changed again as life moved along. I am now enjoying a shift in thinking that most of us old-timers eventually experience - enjoying the simple things like Christmas carols on the radio, hot chocolate with marshmallows, going to Midnight Mass on Christmas Eve, and gathering for a big meal the next day to celebrate the many miracles that are the true reason for the season. I love expressing myself through my Christmas light creations, and I hope you can harness your own sense of hope to **make your next Christmas display something truly special – one that will make memories for your family, friends, neighbors, and strangers, put smiles on people's faces, and help create more hope in the world. One light bulb at a time.**

The Christmas Light
EMPORIUM

www.TheChristmasLightEmporium.com

It is our mission to always be looking for new ways to help Memory Makers create their unique Christmas visions. There are a lot of reasons to shop with The Christmas Light Emporium when bringing your Christmas decorating vision to life. Here are a few:

The Good Stuff (i.e., the stuff you care about most!)

1. **FREE SHIPPING!** On many orders, and most others will qualify for low flat rate shipping of just $7 or $9.

2. **Same**-day shipping on most orders placed by 2 pm Central Standard Time.

3. **Our *Reindeer Proof Warranty*** leads the industry with an average warranty length of 3+ seasons across all product lines.

4. **7 Day Price Protection Policy** means you don't have to worry about waiting for or missing our next big sale. We'll issue a store credit for the different PLUS 10% of the difference if an item you purchase goes on sale at a lower price within seven days after your purchase.

5. **Free return shipping** is available when you choose to exchange or receive store credit as your refund method, and your order includes the low-priced optional Redo returns option.

6. We offer a 30-day return policy (60 days for exchanges or store credit).

7. **Red Suit Rewards customer rewards program**. Earn points for more than just your everyday purchases. It's like Santa leaving you a stocking full of cash on Christmas day!

8. **Easy financing with Shop Pay Installments** - pay over time with no finance charge!

9. **Protect shipments** against loss and theft with *Red Suit Shipping Protection*. When selected with your order - your shipment is protected from loss, damage, and theft. If something happens - *no worries! We'll take care of it for you as quickly as possible.*

10. **We donate a portion of every order to charity** at no cost to you.

BONUS: Our NPS score has been #1 in the holiday lighting industry for seven years running, which means our knowledgeable customer service team is the best!

The Better Stuff (i.e., the stuff we care about most!)

1. We believe in your passion!

2. We are an open book. We truly believe in the hope of the season, and we work hard to provide you with the best products at the best price. We are smaller than some of our competitors, but we sure do work harder to bring you the best experience possible. We will always answer any questions you may have about our business, our products, our people, our pricing, etc., with honesty. This is our open-book policy. We, indeed, are running a business, but it is a business with a mission. That mission is to help you bring more hope into the world. We believe that if you are

a part of this mission, you will help us expand it. And that by providing the best products at a competitive price and with unique and fun perks along the way, we can accomplish this mission together.

3. We are always open to your feedback. This is how we gauge our success (and failures). And it is imperative to our mission.

4. Our customer service is consistently rated among the best in the industry.

5. We use the net promoter score to measure the perceptions of our customers and have held a 5-star net promoter score since inception. In fact, every once in a while, we like to take a look at the keyword cloud that this tool assembles. It is like a website tag cloud but is based on the frequency of words our customers use in their survey responses. It always makes us smile. We aren't perfect, but these visualizations help us see that we are working on point and at least moving toward our mission of helping people share joy and create hope in the world.

TWINKLE! BONUS! – Perks Just for You!

Congratulations! You made it! Now it's time to start planning your path to holiday hero status! Here are some special offers just for you that I hope will save you time and money as you prepare to dazzle your family, friends, neighbors, and the entire galaxy with your extravagant holiday creation!

ChristmasLight
EMPORIUM

COUPON: I *am* biased, but The Christmas Light Emporium is the best place in the universe to shop for everything you need to design and install your dream Christmas display! With everything from **LED bulbs and strings** to **wire-frame displays, greenery**, and every **installation accessory** you will need – The Christmas Light Emporium is your one-stop-shop and *the preferred choice of Memory Makers everywhere.* **www.thechristmaslightemporium.com**

Here's a 15% off code you can use at The Christmas Light Emporium:
TWINKLE-BOOK

Oak & Sugar
CRAFT COCKTAIL MIXERS

BONUS COUPON: I know many of you like to celebrate a job well done. There's no better way to do that than with a Christmas-themed drink from our friends at Oak & Sugar. **www.oakandsugar.com**

Here's a 15% discount code so you can give their **Cherry Bomb Old Fashioned, Holiday Spice Java Martini,** or **Cranberry Glitter Sugar Plum Fairy** a try this Christmas: **TWINKLE-BOOK**

BONUS COUPON: I also know that some of you like to **dress up as Santa and hand out candy** canes to the folks who see your displays. The Costume Emporium carries one of **the world's largest selections of Santa suits**, Mrs. Claus, reindeer, snowman, elf, and other Christmas costumes and accessories. Want to dress up as the famous leg lamp, *"Fragile,"* we can make that happen. www.thecostumeemporium.com

Here's a 15% discount code so you can dress up as your favorite snowman this year: **TWINKLE-BOOK**

I know I told you back in chapter 4 that big fancy light shows are not for the faint of heart, etc. However, if you *DO* decide to give a big, fancy RGB light show a try, here's little gift from our friends at Experience Lights, purveyors of an entire line of advanced RGB light controllers and other great inventions to help you build your wonderland of synchronized lights and music. www.experiencelights.com

Here's a discount code that will get first time customers $25 off any order of $150 or more at experiencelights.com : **TWINKLE-BOOK**

Acknowledgements

There are so many people to thank. Mentors, friends, family, supporters, peers. I will certainly, and without intention, leave out many people who deserve my thanks. I am extremely grateful to a huge number of people for helping me navigate my own decorating journey.

My family: Angela, Sam, and Lauren – for putting up with me all these years

Aaron O'Dell, Andrue Tacina, Brian Holzheuer, Carson Williams, Chuck Smith, Dan & Mary Baldwin, Daniel Kubaczak, Danny Keene, Derek Norwood, George Mosca, Grayson Sanders, Jack Miller, Josh Trees, Katrine Formby, Matt Ellisor, Mike Rentz, Paul Sessel, Ray & Linda Miller, Shawn Tacina

And the old crew, the trailblazers, some of the first extreme decorators around:

Carson Williams, Don Teague, Fabian Gordon, Kevin Judd, Michael Gardner, Richard Holdman, Walter & Jackie Monkhouse

Thank you for your inspiration, your friendship, your mentorship, and your love.

About the Author

Hi. I'm Darren. Nice to meet you :)

I love to travel. I love Christmas. I love starting things. I love music.

These passions have taken me all over the world. From Mt. Everest, to Inland China, a fortified city in Siberian Russia, South America, Africa, Peru, Japan... so many places. I absolutely love traveling the world.

They've also been the catalysts for many commercial undertakings, including Andrew Peripherals, The Big Blue Box, DCX Internet Services, Extreme Lightscapes, The Christmas Light Emporium, The Christmas Light Outlet, The Costume Emporium, Holly Brand Leatherworks, and Oak & Sugar Craft Beverage Co.

And my love for music has never died. I now produce lots of music for other artists and release my own under several project names, including Andrew Caryl, Daz Frydy, and Dilemma Sect. I've worked with artists worldwide, including Venezuelan EDM prodigy Sam Ourt, the immensely talented Melanie Joy Wilpon, and American Idol finalist Robbie Rosen. It continues to be a fun ride.

186

Most recently, I added 'author' to my resume with the publication of this book, Twinkle! The Ultimate Guide To Outdoor Christmas Decorating.

I live in my favorite little city in the world, Denton, Texas, with my wife. Sometimes, my two enormously gifted kids live here with us, too. But they are both off at university most of the time now. I miss them being little. But they make for a couple of awesome humans.

I have a lot of stories. One day, maybe I'll have the time to share them all.

Remember that making memories is the most important job in the world.

Yours truly,
Darren Vader

You can always find me at https://iam.christmas. That's where I'll post new info, updated editions, etc. You will also find helpful tools like drawings, sketches, etc., and reference material for some of the more detailed instructions I've provided in this book. Scan the QR code below to get there quick!